Hotel des Archives

Hotel des Archives

A Trilogy

Chris Tysh

Station Hill Press
BARRYTOWN, NEW YORK

Published by Station Hill Press, the publishing project of the Institute for Publishing Arts, Inc., 120 Station Hill Road, Barrytown, NY 12507, New York, a not-for-profit, tax-exempt organization [501(c)(3)].

Online catalogue: www.stationhill.org

E-mail: publishers@stationhill.org

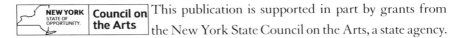 This publication is supported in part by grants from the New York State Council on the Arts, a state agency.

Cover and interior design by Susan Quasha

Library of Congress Cataloging-in-Publication Data

Names: Tysh, Chris, author.
Title: Hotel des Archives : a trilogy / Chris Tysh.
Description: Barrytown, NY : Station Hill Press, [2018]
Identifiers: LCCN 2018022455 | ISBN 9781581771787 (pbk.)
Classification: LCC PS3570.Y65 A6 2018 | DDC 811/.54—dc23
LC record available at https://lccn.loc.gov/2018022455

Manufactured in the United States of America

Contents

To you translators
Thieves and double agents
Who cross time zones
And letter fields
With nothing but
Words in your hands

Preface

Out of the shadowy, always tenuous signs of those "years of lead," to borrow German filmmaker Margareta von Trotte's title, a pool of images haunts me: in peasant skirts, a young woman flees a building while the Gestapo makes its entrance—on a train, caught with a silver tray and taken for a thief, mother murmurs to herself, "better a thief than a Jew"—later, she spit shines the Führer's portrait—May 1945, as the local Nazi obermeister is led in handcuffs between a double hedge of US soldiers, mother and her girlfriend throw him a coat. I see her in her radiant youth, her unbelievable compassion, her hunger to live on. And so I compose a play in verse, *Night Scales, A Fable for Klara K* (United Artists, 2010), a white flag against dying.

After *Night Scales*, which was to a certain degree based on autobiographical material, as it dramatizes my mother's life as a Holocaust survivor and exilic subject in post-war Paris, I very much needed to be engaged in a writing which repudiates the "I" and invest myself in a rather impersonal world. Hence my current zone of interest: translation. The French novels by Samuel Beckett, Jean Genet, and Marguerite Duras offer me the opportunity for a poetic investigation rooted in the voice of the other, which becomes "a reopened language," as Robin Blaser claims, and where the unknown and the outside are let in the gate.

However, I am not talking about a classical exercise of translating, say, Baudelaire's *Les Fleurs du Mal* into English, as Keith Waldrop has done, and sublimely I might add. It is a deterritorialized type of literary translation I've been calling "transcreation" in which I operate a double shift: one of language and genre, as I move from the original French to American and from prose to lyric. Consonant with postmodernism's practice of appropriation and détournement, this tactical move away from ground and origin directs me to writing as a passage or arcade.

Ultimately, transcreation signals to both the first text and its after-life, the graft, that lives on under a new set of linguistic and formal conditions. This regeneration is participatory and dialogic; it prolongs the life of the original like a standard translation does, but at the same time ushers in a gap and a movement away from the generating cell. In ghostly fashion, the new poem is haunted by its French progenitor, while allowing itself to cross over into a totally new temporality and formal structure. This kind of deterritorialized translation is undoubt-edly embedded in postmodernity's vexed stance toward the notion of what passes for originary and authentic. My migratory lyric echoes these contemporary currents of thought.

Samuel Beckett's *Molloy*, written in French and first published by *Les Éditions de Minuit* in 1951, was translated into English by Patrick Bowles, in collaboration with the author and published by Grove Press in 1955. The first volume of a trilogy, along with *Malone Dies* and *The Unnamable*, it is a text wherein the human condition is measured by lack, loss and undoing. But in spite of these dark thematics, Beckett's astounding language grabs us by the throat at the very moment the absurd impossibility of living is affirmed and undone.

In *Molloy: the Flip Side*—the first leg of *Hotel des Archives*—I use Part One of the novel to find a contemporary American vernacular through which the hapless narrator speaks. The three-line stanza compresses the novel's diegetic universe, sparse as it is, and allows me to link the two texts through the projection of a new, speaking subject—a funny, witty, old and disabled bum, going slowly nowhere. "Gotta check out soon / Be done with dying." The result is a poem that opens up the unendurable abyss of being, but whose zany, hobo lyrics keep a beat in a souped-up version of Beckett's existential masterpiece.

In my recasting of the novel *Our Lady of the Flowers*, Jean Genet's 1943 disturbing elegy for social heterogeneity, I attempt to find a poetic equivalent with which to evoke Divine, Mignon-Dainty-Feet, and the young assassin, Our Lady, three saintly figures in a forbidden realm of the senses. The seven-line stanzas of my *Our Lady of the Flowers*, *Echoic* are spacious enough to accommodate the narrative arc, while foregrounding their lyrical impact.

> Under the sheets I choose my nightly
> Outlaw, caress his absent face
> Then the body which resists at first
> Opens up like a mirror armoire
> That falls out of the wall and pins me
> On the stained mat where I think
> Of God and his angels come at last

In Genet, certain indelible images crush us, turning us inside out like a kid glove, sublime moments of inverted logic wherein the quintessentially debased, vile and criminal are canonized, made holy, a savage god: Divine crowning herself with a dental plate; Our Lady strangling the old man; Alberto showing the young Lou a mess of snakes. I lift the originals out of their glass frames and reposition them on a naked table, careful to let the cadences of the line bring out the crystallized word, grafting, suturing in tiny stitches.

The third part of *Hotel des Archives* is devoted to the novel *The Ravishing of Lol V. Stein* by Marguerite Duras, celebrated author of the *Hiroshima Mon Amour* screenplay and winner of the Goncourt Prize for *The Lover*. Duras' book, *Le Ravissement de Lol V. Stein* (Gallimard, 1964), concerns female voyeurism and the complex logic of desire. Her admittedly always-already poetic narrative is carried into prosody as a mode of expression, that without entirely losing the novel's ribbon of events, travels along its border and yet always retains the libidinal shadow that haunts her lines. The couplet, that arch classic measure, seems perfectly designed to carry Duras' ineffable music and, in particular, to gesture at the phantasmic nature of a couple.

But like a hyphen between
knowing and unknowing

there and there
I continue my descent

with a fist of ifs
and maybes

If you ask why these three novels, you're right to ask. It could eas-
ily have been those of Sartre, Beauvoir and Camus, or else Bataille,
Blanchot and Leiris, or say, earlier in the century, Breton, Aragon and
Soupault, all equally vital in terms of French cultural capital. But truth
be told, the ones I've picked offer themselves as sites of carrying out a
certain sense of otherness, a critical encounter with subjectivity that is
cross-hatched by lack, degradation and/or gender dissent, which have
always hailed me as particularly indispensable to my understanding of
the world from a position of non-mastery. "Fail better," as the Becket-
tian motto goes. Whether it is Molloy staggering through the mire on
the way to mother, or Divine approaching the season of tears, or Lol
stretched out in a field of rye spying on a pair of lovers, each one elicits
a kind of empathy that transforms the question of being.

More than just fundamental literary archives of the French *pat-
rimoine*, for me these texts materialize the very notion of alterity, of
being the other, *l'étranger,* the sexual pariah, the female voyeur: the
Irishman writing in the langue of Racine, the con man dreaming of
young assassins, the woman jilted at the municipal ball. To fold these
bodies and images into song is my siren's call.

CHRIS TYSH
Detroit, 2017

Molloy: The Flip Side

ESTRAGON: Off we go again.

—Samuel Beckett

In a din chamber
Mother sets my vice
A little bed of needles

I have no fucking idea
How I got here
Someone called 911

Ma's aide, maybe
Sent him a strong current
Checked the floor for balance

He swears "no way"
Hands over a few bucks
And picks up the stack

Tinfoil, tin darts. We jet
And unravel evidence
A nest of imports, so they say

What's what now: speak!
Gotta check out soon
Be done with dying

While they read the signs
Parrot's mess, a broken sink
My legs bid adieu

Who am I kidding? Haven't done
Squat in weeks, can't read
His chicken scrawl; he barks "why not?"

I write "mortar" for "mortal"
Without wanting to correct
My mistake like a stranger

In a dark forest I piss on words
"Vase," "bed," same struggle
Only plusher. A relation of sorts

I spawned one somewhere
He'd be an old fart now
Not the grand love you're right

See a pretty bonnet, a crumb
I lifted her rug, so tiny
And slanted toward a door

If I'm not mistaken
I've known him, my son, that is,
Crap! I forget his name again

The question bars my way
Every stump every bit of damp
Muck wants to be born

All goes blank. Any minute now
I'll go bat blind, then the head
An empty pot will follow

Pain's IOUs stick in my throat
Where they make a fist as if
To say we'll show you

Did you say what I think
I heard? Fault? Boo-boo, blunder
Slipup? Do you still use such slurs?

At this moment, peep holes
Like troughs drain light
Leaky little eaves in the bed of the sea

Then neither tavern nor black weeds
Only A and B in an empty field
Till the cow drags its ass home

It's the fixity of the empty set
A bit self-conscious of standing in
For twisty bleak road ahead

No doubt about it. There were two
Of them; they had just met in a ditch
Wearing coats because of the weather

The brute mezzo of stomping feet
Beneath means nothing yet
But at dawn they'll speak some

It's not like they're buddies
Waiting for a pint or a handshake
On the way to the office

The treason of hills
Finds a path no doubt
From his bedroom

Where he guesses
Flanks, crests and valleys
Rise, indigo even

Even if it were the caverns
Of his heart—that black
Crevasse he roams at night

Pressing his stick, I'm ashamed
To say, once level and stout
Now a mere shadow where I crouch

But this cigar in the breach
Like a corkscrew in my guts
Sand, ashes and dust of fallen things

The fuming hand, mangy skin; alright,
I stink. My crutches scrape as I try to
Ask him, please, the this and that

East of history, I missed stuff
The very alphabet, a large glass
Somebody left in the alley

Shit! I hate talking about myself
Since every I is a he. Look, he split!
Should I be watching him still?

To row in silence toward
The world of objects is to wish
A story resembled them but better

Whereas I'm at bottom
I mean literally, that's my crib
Somewhere between scum and mire

B, isn't it? Among chariots
And the rah-rah of carts leaving
Town before dawn; it could happen

Then a series of bangs taps out
Next part, fraps as with ropes or cables
Nightly mares that race mad around the bend

I wonder what the hell that means
Let's blow this joint—I've got places
To be—my mother's, to be blunt about it

No need to remark a certain blue
Hour when I mount the shaky
Premise I'll call hereafter a bike

And don't ask me how I tie my crutches
Nor how I pedal with one leg—slightly
Less stiff than the other—ah! the little red horn

Who gives a rat's ass! Who hears
The crakes' awful racket in the grain
Fields, a chain of events I imagine

Within the strict compass
Of my journey caked with
Darkness, sans sex sans parent

The thing is mother and I—
My shitty start—are so old now
We're like two sere fucks on a rail

Dilapidated ma, Mag
Hello, Caca Countess!
Poor fit of flesh and bone

We'll skip the introductions
Go straight to the empty sweep
Of eyes, knobby knees pressed

Together and the manic lift
Of her dentures: a short rap to
The skull means yes, no, maybe

I mime the answers with my hands
Lest she mix up the banknotes
For that crust of bread she shoves in

It's not her money I'm after
Gray soft sac and yet I'll crawl
Back like a mugger in the night

But enough about her! Let's go
To the funky road bazaar at the
Edge of town, purple flowers

A little further on, mark the way
Vats and papers in the traffic isle
Like pastry doilies I vaguely think

Oh no! The copper wants the other
Paper with my mug on it; it's the law
He says for richer or poorer, lame or not

Up to the station we must go; I remember
That much—the air is kind under the blue
Sky of the policeman's eye

Could it be the quarter
Of slaughterhouse, gaslight
And blunt instruments?

Forget about it! I told you
I have blanks in this area
Minus the fact I'm dying

To sit down although
It's a canned image
Blue and gold from before

The somber soil saw a crisscross
A fan of figures from liquid
To coarse crooks shuffling in place

In the aha moment that follows
I blurt out "Molloy's the name"
Sure I'm sure, Mr. Commissar

Roughly speaking though free
To go I understood my body's
Dumb trespass on decency

Does nothing to ease the long
Theory I sit on like an abandoned
Subway station, toothless and lost

To the world of putrid chairs
Blanched façade and the hazy
Cut-out of me and my bike

All that nonsense at the precinct
Like kicking a dead horse
Excites my hunger big time

Hold on! Now comes the famous
Passage of sucking stones I move
From pocket to mouth and back again

A suggestion of cinnamon
Passes my senses, the most
Stranded of organs left high and dry

Hobbling I make for the ditch's
Empty bed under white hawthorn
A fistful of grass on my tongue

Take it easy, pal! You can
Still spread your toes and hear
The wind howl. It's not over

Till the fat lady sings or the flies buzz
Or someone draws the blinds
Or whatever the fuck that's scary

It's not that eerie hour's martyr light
Nor the stone remains of a house
In the slow effacement of a name

But just before a singular night
There by the side of a canal
Full of shadows against my thoughts

Which trail off like comet ends
Having already done their share
Of fixing the thin rain that falls

In this regard the long caravan
Begins with a barrage like a wedding
Band pushing their way through

Whether it's sheep or donkeys
The shepherd whistles the same
Tune for his collie who runs ahead

Past the final destination. I'm afraid
I won't know for sure how it all
Goes for the little creatures above

A certain angle, mimetic at that,
The body's pulse crashes like a glass
Jar against the familiar ramparts

In the case of my hometown
Surely as splendid as any other
I read about, something strange

Holds me aloof from its name:
Goddamn! Does it start with a B
Or what? Please, lady, somebody?

Pour me a noun, a sensation
I recognize, a knitted form
Spreads out its venom letters

Made of scraps and copper
Wires I loop around like a veil
For the anonymous hack (that'd be me)

You fool! Do you even remember
The words "true or false" in the parlance
Of this dead world's icy curse?

A shorthand for the long sonnet
Where echoes die with a smile
On their cadaver lips

And I make a beeline
For the nearest outhouse
Without once looking

Who's straddling who—all things
Not being equal—there will be
Hell to pay later

It is understood apart from
My tendency to fall dead
Against a passerby who happens

To take Teddy—old, deaf and
Incontinent—be done with
His suffering as they say

Kindly. Had I run over
Her dog, the constable asked
To make a long story short, Miss

Loy or Lousse, first name Soph,
Saved my nubby neck with her
Matching silver voice

It's a stretch to compare
The rest to velvety flesh
Hidden in a web of gray folds

In exchange I'm to help her
Bury the cold yellow mutt
Under a tree, it's customary

The same might be said
About me or her parrot
Which now screams "Fuck!

Son of a bitch" instead of
"Pretty Polly," the lady wants
To complete the fantasy

Like a plain cracker, cheesy
And futile I crumple in the
Penumbra of her chambers

My crutches are elsewhere
And my beard's shaven
Little fork of questions

I doubt I will lift in the air
No more than the dumb short
Nightie covering my balls

That the answer might
Pour from the front lobe
Is more par for the course

I'm not a perfume expert
But it seems someone has
Dabbed me with lavender

Extract. Might as well
Put me on the chopping
Block like a virgin or a wife

From the east fits of lunacy
See to it I have nothing but
A tiny patch of securities

As a rule the moon is a cunt
Waltzing slowly left to right
Leaving long stripes on the wall

Of that madwoman's attic or
That other nutcase with the yellow
Wallpaper I too would rip to shreds

It's hard to speak of ruins
Without the eternal alarm
Setting off our hearse clip-clop

Give up the ghost now or
Later someone yells in my ear
As I close my eyes at once

Cupped hand like a crown
Of flames flashes white
From one stiff to another

Speaking of native ground
Before the fracas of death
Is it possible that the time

Elapsed between that first
Eve I spied my two thieves
A fortnight ago has gone missing?

The ceiling's empty dome
Beaded with false color
Adds up to my absence

I won't say more about it
It resembles nothing so much
As the ephemeral drenching light

That parts the novel's pages
Down to the shaft one could
Just call a perfect cube, penciled in

Where the hell are my clothes
I scream at the clueless valet
Shaking my crutches for emphasis

To tell the truth I didn't really
Scream nor shake my fists
But sometimes I can't help

Miming would be the word
The very contours like a thin
Smooth envelope others call life

On the other side of the ledger
Inspection reveals a loose
Spring in the sum total, a hole

Where my possessions had been
Hat, bicycle, sucking stones
Slow boat to nowhere

But I'll be damned if I leave
Them my knife. Out with it
Now, minion, meat puppet!

Can't bear to suffer
The distant mess—cut
To a leg—barefaced lie

Or dim-witted phrase
Take your pick. There's
Always the ache of sameness

A bundle latched
Close to the vest
Pending one's arrest

If I now at last speak
Of the immodest proposal
Goody Lousse entertained

It's only fair to take in the whole
Scene in her garden: I stretched out
Like a dog and she of the flounces

Pouring debauch's demands
Nary a tuft of grass between us
Hunched over the hemmed space

From the get-go I say yes to
The grub and the other tango
Of her clever plot and yet

A shudder escapes me like
A fallen log or shoelace
Free from its tongue

As is my wont upon this night
Of echoes this menu of bruises
The earth spits up along the way

Having dismissed the two
Clowns who always crash
Inside my padded skull

Or rather having done
One's bidding before
The other can say "boo"

In the putative nest
We move to as if in a fable
Of leaves and petals

That make up my jar
Stopped with rags
And safe from seasons

All this adds up to diddly-
Waddle which explains
The itsy bitsy spider in my eye

Not much of a key to open
Darkness' till or cash in on
The shipwreck in its wake

That this period existed
For real, fuck if I know
As the schoolboys like to say

That I stayed with the old bag
A little while or a year remains
Buried in the yard, naught but bones

I slap myself out of my cup
Return from falling down
Like a disowned son a doll

In the crook of his arm
The meal all proper
On a round red tray

I tear into the food
Cric-crac I'm done
Like a savage

That is, if I'm at the gate
Else I go hungry for days
5 mugs of beer in my gullet

On the assumption that
Regret's eerie map is best
Left behind I slip through

To the long corridor of now
No more than a cage for the crazy
Flap-flap-glide of this chapter

I better stop spitting on the titty
Of my existence—do you even
Hear yourself—just close your trap

On the score of Lousse's estate
Can't bear the sight of her open
Mouth and that B-flat chest of hers

What's her story? Man, woman
Who cares? Speaking of flat
My first one, Ruth or Edith

If I recall was one of them
I mean a woman with a slit
She taught me how in spite

Of her bad back and rough
Ebony cane. Was that real love
That blinking light that exile

Passing for tenderness
Trembling jelly I know full well
Such frothing and yellowed skin

Detoured from their path
Her cane upon my fly
What pandemonium each time

Under our panic jolts
The narrow cot moved all
By itself like a phantom

In a vacant lot where we'd met
I would've shagged a goat
Thus the wretched force of nature

It was a short fling though
She kicked the bucket soon
After, a quiet death in her tub

I suspect with slim evidence
Mister, mistress, same difference
The least of my worries now

This very evening crammed
With double traces, understudies
For that single hag flattened

Out on the stones like a revenant
Truth be told I finally pulled
The door without a word or sign

Profiting from the fact
My hostess eyed her flowered
Pet grave, I depart sans bike

Into another world
Wind, stars and night sky
For companions

After wandering until dawn
I find a refuge of sorts
In a blind alley, really a recess

A jetty it was not unless one
Count the sea of excrements
Piling up in their raw state

Did I say I tried to slit my wrist
Without much gusto, it seems
Just a compulsion to repeat

Certain gestures, their small
Wings dip down against the wind
A deficit only death can suspend

This vein this ridge this line
Of thinking more trouble than
It's worth; the old levee won't

Go bust just yet. In any case
I was finally out in the open
Air, a handful of silver spoons

Swiped; I can't put my finger
On why. Hence the riddles and
Long divisions into dark columns

A series of rattles and foul
Impressions bring us up to
Speed—call it a pirouette

An enjambment that straddles both
Old specters and night shrouds,
And *the rosy-fingered dawn*

A matter of poking a hole
In the drapes; first my hands
Which are hardly ever mine

Then the feet with their own
Verdict—let's not forget them—
End of citation, I mean flashback

Off we go on the stroke
Of the city clock hiding
In plain sight; nothing's

More dangerous than
Just before noon when
All good folks check

Their doorways for rats
And the three fresh stripes:
Order, justice and beauty

I make myself scarce then
Melting into walls like a cat
Until the shadows grow

Careless and I land dead
Tired and bowed by my habit
To crawl on hands and knees

I find that blackish crack
In the earth and draw apart
Its walls, less rat than mole

Just because I'm scribbling
In this notebook doesn't mean
I have to tell you where and what

And even though it would
Make a pretty picture I better not
Recount my blue period by the sea

And don't imagine diamond
Depths, distant isles, reefs nor
Surf I weathered in my skiff

Perish the thought! Here begins
The other round trip from one pocket
To the other, a carousel of rocks

I divvy up in four piles exactly
Between my pants and my coat
Left-right-mouth-hand-and-back

It wasn't that hard to keep
Shuffling the deck of stones
As it were. Move, cries the cop

Inside my head while I suck—
God forbid—the same four
Pebbles or worse, just one

In the end I throw the whole
Lot up in the air hoping to save
One but even *that* I lose or swallow

There you have it! We're all nothing
But a dark point on this wild coast
Who would want to hurt us?

The weirdest thing—I see better
At the beach—all that vast sandy
Flatness makes my good eye

Work harder. Even stranger
I can name the black specks
Drifting in the distance, yes!

A woman is coming towards
Me in the terrible grave of this
Shore seeming to freeze midway

Like a caryatid on a ship's prow
Arms lifted bearing torches
Or driftwood the poor collect

After a storm but maybe
I'm thinking of another time
Anterior—I give up the pretense

To stitch this impossible tale
In its proper order: what comes
After might as well be a gate

I count back from more or less
Sloshing through old debris
Mother's image like a filigree

Pattern, twisted threads black
On gold that involuntary
Memory plaits out of nowhere

As far as I can remember
There's always been a swamp
And I'm not being metaphorical

Between my town and the sea
And hardly a year goes by
When a vast harbor plan

With canals docks and public
Works isn't hatched and let go
Palace walls in one hand

Spongy tract in the other
Just enough black water
To drown the innocent

It is not false to claim
That my progress—if
One can call it that—

Is a total bust given
My *good* leg just for kicks
Has gone numb and stiff

As if not to be in debt
To the other limb which
Takes the rap in stride

Well, fuck a duck! I don't
So much mind the old pail
Of nerves and tendons

Supposed to be lame and
Growing shorter by the second
But what pisses me off no end

Is the pillar the pivot I'm leaning
On now decides after all to ape
Its poor chum: stagger, shuffle, crawl

A worm would go faster than us
Besides whether the legs labor
Or go on strike, their pain remains

"Present" when the master calls
Attendance on the narrow lanes
Veiled in fog

Should we wish to go on
The only way will be to stop
At random—no cross no calvary—

But still I wonder
I have that caprice
Will I ever see the day

Strung out on a thread
Between these giant fronds
Never mind I hated its very guts

Before. And my mother, could
She still be waiting for me?
Shouldn't I instead slip

A knot on a branch
Or better yet just slash
My throat?

As it happens all ideas
Of suicide don't hold
A candle to my stump

In the silent night
I wrap a coat around
My head like a Berber herdsman

To muffle the dreadful
Death rasp I pass off
As a coughing jag

To say that my progress
Was slowing down
Doesn't even come close

To the facts I'll be kind
Enough to mention now
Who says "weak points"

Has a leak in his tank
Button missing a hole
In his wig, you feel me?

It's the speed of going
To sticks and dogs
Since I left the seashore

That I didn't bargain on
Then, if I felt my own bunghole
I couldn't have said, "OOO

It's much worse off than yesterday!"
I beg your pardon for coming back
To this shameful dark county

Such a bad rap!
An injustice if you ask me
Squeezed, passed in silence

And contempt when it's more
A hyphen in the spelling of the world
Our being's truest portal, it seems

And the famous mouth? History
Asks. Nothing but a service door
Left ajar. You do the math

Let's be perfectly clear
At the beach my so-called
Limbs nod to their fall

In a strict rhythm
Nothing to write home
About but no sooner

Than I find myself
On the open roads
Damn toes decide to call

It quits. For sure
We're peering into the same
Cabinet of inconvenience

Sorry leg story: corns
Bunions, cramps, the whole
Ingrown grief dictionary

Definition of pain
In the ass; as it were
My weaknesses lay elsewhere

Still. One ought to map them
Out like a new territory
With faint blue lines

For all liquid states
I swear I can hardly
Piss nowadays

And then a strong red
For the heart that beats
No matter what

Ah the bitch, she sure as hell
Passed me them rotten genes
How did she croak already?

Who knows! Maybe they buried the old bag
Alive. Might as well wring *my* sponge too
Give up the putative fence link to the rest

As I index all my pros and cons
Listen for the bell or start gun
To tell me it's the end of the line

Last stop! Everyone off the bus!
There's something strained
In these transport metaphors

So poorly attuned to my station
But for now I must stress
There were days when my legs

Had to be higher than my head
Not an easy task with stiff
Planks and the dark forest carpet

For a bed. Thirty, at most
Forty steps is all I could
Muster at times, hardly

A barrel coming through
The white waters or a buzzard
Taking flight

Naturally I told myself
The blue penumbra
It was not green as one

Would assume, things
Are due their pound of flesh,
Absorbed the red sun

And the green of leaf, at least
That's how I reasoned the blue
Gloom that now kept me going

So to speak—what savages you are
My little vocabs! Picture then
A square, a crossroads, a ring

As one can find in the deepest
Forest at times. I'm talking
Shafts of light like a gate

Or storefront in the middle
Of nowhere. Say, no wonder
I stagger in my mind to the coal-

Man I met there—woods
Will do that to you—
Any shelter, stray dogs happen

Had I been seventy
Years younger maybe
I could've loved him

When I was no taller
Than a stack of apples
My preference went to

Old men, I do believe
I had time for one or two
Not like the grand passion

Absolutely nothing to do
With the old one—what's
Her name—Rose? You know

Who I mean but still
A tenderness breaking
Open in the forgotten earth

But now I hate the rotten
Lot: ripe or not, piss me off
The nerve! He, a perfect

Stranger, in the illness of solitude,
Begging me to share his hut
Coalman, my butt! I see no smoke

Get me out of here I say
With the right words
In the right order

Though once more I can't
Put my finger on the name
Of my hometown

The man had never been out
Of the woods where he was born
The more eloquent I become

The less he understands
Trolling for my sleeve
The old pervert!

In a flash I let my crutch
Rap him one upside the head
Boom! He's quiet now!

Thus I continue on my way
But before long I do a uwie
To check his vitals

Given that he's still breathing
A few sweet kicks in the ribs
Do the trick, a falling backwards

For me each time I miss my shot
Having aimed too low
Something soft beneath my heel

Most likely a kidney
Not enough force to crack
Open, definitely not

Just because folks are old
Poor, lame and scared shitless
Doesn't mean we can't defend

Our fortress, though that may be
True as a rule but under certain
Conditions, faced with an attacker

Who is all thumbs, a retard, pretty
Much my size and in a forsaken
Place, one is sometimes permitted

To show the wood, mettle or stuff
We're capable of. That'd be the only
Reason I linger on this dumb incident

To recall such a possibility
Too often forgotten like all
Tales that teach or caution

Was I even eating then?
Sure, a thing or two
Roots, slugs, carobs

You'd think I was a goat
Pecking and pawing
The underbrush for crumbs

Had I once heard or
Read that in a forest
If you go straight north

You end up walking in circles?
Please note how well I retain
Whenever I take the trouble

In accordance I do my best
To go round and round
Hoping to find my way

Out of the woods through
This reverse logic day after
Day I push on, if not strictly

In a straight line, at least
I'm not making circles
Like a spinning top

Or wheel that's fallen
Off a truck; that's something
Because I'm not married

To the forest; my name's
Not Remus or Romulus for
Crying out loud; wasn't suckled

By a she-wolf that's for sure
There's more to see like plains
Mountains and rivers, must be

Towns and villages strapped
To roads and highways
I'm out of here, snap

Because I've done it before
More than once. Granted
Things were different then

Raining down from on high
Hope has me squint at the strange
Light wafting pale like a whim-wham

On the flat plain I know I'll see
Some day. Still stiff with doubt
I figure at least I know what's

What in the woods. Perforce
Its amenities where I'm concerned
Take the cake since I'm here

And not there if you follow
My peculiar way of grasping
Things. All I mean to say

Is that being already there
In the forest, that is, and free
To stay—no small item

Between my legs and the
State of this piteous body—
Turns me around in my leafy bed

A person is, mind you,
More than a wad of tissues
Bones and joints propped

Against the stiff boughs
Of the night. Who goes
Whispering in my ears

Like a stage prompter
His name is "Imperative"
That's different I think

Without voice waiting for
The pattern to make sense
Truth be told I submit

At your service, have no
Idea why, since more often
Than not, the said imperatives

Have never landed me
In a good spot, even worse
Black radish of a fact

Have always torn me
Away from places which
Though not necessarily great

Happened to be a stop a rest
Only to leave me stranded
On the seat of my pants

That ring of imperatives
An old habit by now
I confess follows a single path

Bordered by need's blackthorn
The very same indelicate
Matter of my mother

Come to think of it
They all sing the same
Couplet. I can hear

The warning if I lean in
Closer: Leave the forest
At once or it might be

Already too late
Did I speak Latin?
The quoted ditty

Seemed to think so
Thank you kindly
"Nimis sero"

At bottom the voice
Wasn't the only culprit
I sound out the words

But always something else
Holds me back. Molloy,
Forget about it!

Wasn't the command
Calling me to order
Now loud like a tooth-

Ache now softly dying
As if to say nothing good
Can come of it

And did I, of all people,
Need apostrophes now
Whispering now shouting

As I have mentioned
More than once
The better to show

Really to ridicule
The spun wool of
My hesitancy?

When in fact, the whole time
I had been going, methinks
Since my first milk tooth

Toward mother
So as to nail the frame
Of our relation on a less

Wobbly table, broken
Glass underhand
The story gets weirder

By the minute: Having
Arrived and I did manage
That many a time

I would scramble slap-bang
Or to be more exact
Stir my stumps

Without having done a thing
And far away from her
I would again be en route

Hoping to do better
Next time, ants in my pants
I would travel as if squeezed

By a chain pulling little
Sleds in my dome
Till drained and half-starved

I gave the appearance
A portrait in sum
Of someone who could give

A fuck (gasp!) where she was
And yet in reality did nothing
Else but plot and scheme

Better ways to find my way
To her house. Soon enough
At the rate I'm going

It will be a moot point
This train of thinking
This eternal seesaw

This monkey mind
I would have to stay put
Or be carried on a stretcher

You must realize by now
That when I say a voice
Told me, Molloy, do this

Or that, followed by a clear
Elegant sentence I'm only
Bowing to convention's noose

Which spells the cardinal rule
Cook up a story or hold your tongue
For the whole package, I mean

The true realm of things
Happened quite differently
Between you and me

I wasn't saying crap
But I heard a rumor
Something eerie about

That silence. All ears I'd
Listen like a possum
Startled and pretending

To be dead. From deep
Inside although muffled
Some sort of conscience

Would rise up in me
Which I now translate
From memory

By saying Molloy
Don't do a thing…
It seems as though…

Or I had the impression of…
Nothing but figures
Of speech, lying white sheep

Be as it may, though
I formed absolutely
No impression whatsoever

There was something new
Somewhere that meant I had
To change or the world at large

Or else all remain the same.
And it is these very small
Adjustments like Galileo's vessels

I'm trying to express
With silly phrases
I'm afraid that

I was hoping for
Surely if I really tried
I could've spoken

Otherwise, with more
Shape and truth
Oracle mouth

As for the breaks
They were getting
Longer and longer

One can scarcely speak
Of marches much less
Having a leg up

In the spongy dark ground
Where my crutches sank
Neither living nor dead

It must've been winter
Blue shadows like maiden
Hair hung from the black

Branches, almost trembling
Under leaden skies
Fact is the slushy leaves

Slowed me down but even
Without the sludge I would
Renounce walking like men

I'll never forget the day
When defying the rules
Flat on the earth

A message flashed
On the screen of my brain:
One can always crawl, damn it!

Wait! First I need to talk
About the forest's sounds
Everyone knows the hunting

Horn goes well together
In a sort of spiffy way
It's expected, but a gong!

A tom-tom wouldn't
Shock me half as much
What a pity to hear nothing

But a gong in the far
Distance when one pines
For the famous hum

No doubt I might confuse
It with my heart for just a sec
Though you'd be better off

Bringing in hydraulics
To explain the noise
That old pump makes

I listen to the leaves
Now stiff and silent
As if cast in brass

So much for murmurs
In the woods, the moon
And the pose of hearing

From inside my pocket
I'd press the soft pear
Of my bicycle horn

An owlet could hoot
Louder! And now
Let's be done already.

Flat on my belly
Crutches thrust
In the underbrush

I pull myself forward
As if they were studs
Lucky my wrists are still

Strong though swollen
With arthritis the kind
That knits a bushel of roses

For your bony mitts
Maybe quite obvious
This mode of locomotion

Has the distinct advantage
When it comes to rest
You just stop exactly

As you are, boom! It's done
Some are known to move
About sitting or even kneeling

Pulling left and right
Forward and backward
They got it down to a science

And thus I did my twenty
Steps a day in the forest
Without killing myself for it

Eyes half-closed
On black clumps
Against the sky

I would even crawl
Blindly on my back
A human puddle, no less

I'm going to mom's!
Every so often I'd
Say "mom" to give

Myself courage
While my hat
Which had lost

Its strap would fly
Away with each thrust
Until I rammed it hard

So far down it stuck
Forever on my skull
Had I met some dames

I'd be at pains
To salute them
Like a gentleman

You will remember
That in my mind
Which worked

But quarter time
I needed to go
Round and round

So that every third
Or so ramp, having
Revised my course

I'd end up describing
If not a circle
A vast polygon

To each his portion of
Shredded mince pie
Letting me believe

In spite of all that I was
Moving in a straight line
Day and night to mother's

And then came the day
The forest stopped
Just as I knew it would

Aquiver beyond the grave
Tree trunks the plain light
Ahead is how I imagined

The scene and yet
I'm telling you
I just happened to open

My eyes and there it was
I had arrived
For Christ's sake!

This surely can be explained
For some time now
I only opened my eyes

Once in a blue moon
All the little creep
Maneuvers I did in the dark

As the forest ends in a ditch
That is where I must've
Fallen for why else would I

Keep my eyes open?
Like an endless sea
The plain rolled on

Far on the horizon
Could it really be?
I fancied towers and steeples

There's no betting
It was my city until
Further notice

Truly the plain
Seemed familiar
Don't get me wrong

It's like a god box
You've seen one
You've seen all

Whether this was hometown
Or not, whether these faint
Fumes my mother breathed

Or stank up the place
A hundred miles from here
Was beside the point

For someone in my position
Though not without its merit
In terms of pure knowledge

How was I supposed to haul
My carcass over this green stuff
Where my crutches groped in vain

Rolling like a ball?
Would they let me roll
To mother's very stoop?

Help's on the way
I vaguely heard
Cross my heart

These words exactly
Loud and clear
Like the time I stopped

A kid's marble
Thanks a lot he'd said
Not to worry, Molloy

We're coming. Jesus!
What in the world!
I just roll to the bottom

It must've been spring
Seems like birds were
Chirping maybe skylarks

Hadn't I heard them before
In the woods? By the sea?
Perhaps gulls? Couldn't say

For sure. I remember land
Rails. The two travelers
Come to mind. One had a club

I had forgotten about them
I see the sheep again.
Bah, that's what I say now

Stop worrying. Other scenes
Of my life were coming back
It seemed to me that it was

Raining and then sunny
One after the other
Typical spring weather

I felt like going back
Into the forest
Mind you, not like dying

To go but a little itching
Palm. After all, Molloy
Could stay where he was.

Our Lady of the Flowers, Echoic

*To be decapitated is to appear—banded, erect: like the
"head swathed" (Weidmann, the nun, the aviator, the
mummy, the nursling) and like the phallus, the erectile
stem—the style—of a flower.*

—Jacques Derrida

On the news Weidmann, his head
Like a nun in white or a wounded
Pilot, falls down in silky rye
The same day Our Lady of the Flowers
Stamped all over France dangles his crimes
By a golden string—nimble assassins mount
The back stairs of our sleep

There were others, of course, orphaned
Fragments I overhear prisoners sing
Inside when voices rise in psalm
From the depth of their misery
Each time my heart bangs like it did
When the German dropped his bomb
And I smiled, a tiny sign between us

It can't be pure chance that I cut out
Those handsome heads with empty
Eyes or rather sky-blue windows
On the construction site not yet up
Who said vacant? When their eyes do close
It's creepier than a viper's nest to the girl
Who walks by the barred spy-hole

That each cell becomes where strange types
Crash, swear and dream on straw pallets
Or maybe something of a confession
Booth with its dark screen. Empty
Theatres, deserted prisons, idle machinery
Those eyes hold me entranced and I feel
My way, groping along like a blind man

Until in wild panic I arrive by a sordid alley
Face to face with nothing but a void
Propped and swollen like a huge foxglove
The papers torn, sheared of their pimps
Like a May garden looted of its blossoms
It is you I remember at night: stretched
Like a coffin at sea, pale and wintry

You flow into me, white blessed body
Now a halo, supernatural cocoon
You prick with both your feet.
Out of chewed bread I make glue
For my cutouts—some I pin with brass wire
That inmates use for funereal wreaths
Now star-shaped frames for the criminal

Element. I live here among ruins
Smiles or pouts all enter through
My open pores, myself, my family.
To give them their due, their retinue
I've added a few profiles from those
Cheap paperbacks we smuggle in the yard:
Young half-breed or Apache with a hard-on

Under the sheets I choose my nightly
Outlaw, caress his absent face
Then the body which resists at first
Opens up like a mirror armoire
That falls out of the wall and pins me
On the stained mat where I think
Of God and his angels come at last

With the help of my unknown lovers—
Nobody can say when and if I'll get out—
I'll compose a story: my heroes are
Stuck on the wall and I in lock-down
As you read about Divine and Culafroy
You might at times hear lines mixed in
With a drop of blood, an exclamation point

In the drowsy morning as the screw
Throws in his low "Bonjour"
The fact of a few pink girls, now white
Corpses, flows through
An ineffable fairytale I tell
In my own words
For the enchantment of my cell

Divine died yesterday
In a pool of blood more red
You would see Jesus' oriflamme
Flying for The Sacred Heart
Her lungs like a piece of evidence
In the judge's chamber squeezed shut
Now it rains behind bars, wind too

A spiral stairway leads to the attic
Overlooking a small Montmartre
Cemetery where D lived for a spell
It will be the anteroom of her crypt
Thick with putrid flowers and incense
Floor to floor it rises toward death
And then at the top no more

Than a phantom shadow
Tinged with blue while outside
Let's say under the black canopy
Of tiny umbrellas, Mimosa I,
Mimosa II, Mimosa half-IV,
First Communion, Angela, Her
Highness, Castagnette and Régine

Await holding sprays of violets
All the queens, boys and girls
Are there knotted together chattering
And tweeting, pearl tiaras on their heads
I let myself sink to my old village grave-
Yard where snails and slugs leave
Trails of slime on white flagstones

"Poor darling!" "Can you beat it?"
"She was losing it." "Where's Mignon?"
Any minute now there'll be a black-horse
Procession and the rest by way of Rachel
Avenue. Oh the scene! The Eternal makes
His entrance, smiling, supple and elegant
Without a hat. They call him Mignon-Dainty-Feet.

In the rectangle of my door I thought
I saw him once like a dead man walking
On pricey furs. In a flash, I'm his
Discharged to the core—not a dab of self
Remains but ruffian, pimp and gangster
He's lodged instead, his lacy fingers—
Baby Jesus in its crib—receive the world

As he moves through the queens
Like a shiny slaughterhouse knife
They part and recast in silence
Their traveling line—two at a time
He runs up the steps, lifted, I'd have
Said, to the house of death now real
As tears, flowers and mourning veil

Old Ernestine, Divine's mother
Though still a beauty was done for
Having ransacked a thousand and one
Roles from pulp novels that corrupt
The real: gun in gloved hand
She stages her son's dénouement
The way others shoot up smack

With a crystal spike
The room slides like a diamond
On her index finger into gold
Velvet and walnut-paneled walls
"I feel it, Lou's hour has come,"
She moans using the boy's old name
Buried axe at the bottom of a pool

The whole construction bound
To shatter her nerves, feeling faint
Amid hangings, beveled mirrors
And gloom's infernal ruckus
In two seconds flat, she recovers her cool
Would go first lighter than thought
And wait by the coffin, gray shape now

That's how Mignon saw her
Drunk with grief like a Queen
Of Spades, black widow of dry
Wings spread across the bed
Curtains, walls and rugs that wear
Death's private seal stamped low
On the parchment. Some stray dogs

Like to repeat such news, scent of sulfur
In the air—already Mignon forgets the pad
He shared with D, will not linger near the lacy
Shroud. He's simply drifting about.
Outside, a black cortège, rouge and blush
Finally arrives by the pit already dug
And Divine is no more: dead and buried

Among cries and girly giggles.
Divinaria, D's saga, will be the tale
I trace in the starless subterranean sky
Switching genders as if passing under
A nightclub's scarlet awning where I steal
A glance at some elfin gypsy with hair
Covered in dew and river marsh

Limpid water to the shapeless mud of others
Divine enters Graff's café at two a.m.
Fresh scent of scandal at her heels
Heads turn: bankers, gigolos and scarecrows
Her public life starts now: alone at a table
A ceremony with black tea and a pair
Of pants stolen from a sailor.

Her seduction will be implacable
Finer than amber and yet she's kin
To the prowlers at fairgrounds
Who with a flick of their wrists
Set slot machines and trail behind them
The fatal lacework of magic city
She crosses her legs and smiles

She's cruising tonight and no dice
If it were up to me I'd give her marble
Hips, polished cheeks and pagan knees
From which to climb toward Pigalle
Picture her on a bench, a hint of leg
And a column of smoke rising
"They're crazy about me, those nights

Oh the sultanas! My God, they're
Tickling my ass, the cheeky girls."
Some mornings, men wake up gasping
So horny they'd swallow their own hand
To be done with wanting. Divine is hungry
In the empty streets only a few rowdy teens
Insert a stripe of sound, undone shoelaces

Dragging behind. It's understood
She won't score tonight. Just then
A man bumps into her. "I'm so sorry."
"No problem," says the queen. It is
Mignon-Dainty-Feet: 5'9", 165 lbs, blond,
Blue-green eyes, perfect teeth, oval face,
10-inch prick, and as young as D

When I knew her in the joint at Fresnes
She'd talk about him, deep swell prone
To exaggerate the sumptuous contours
Of his face I never met in person and now
Must borrow a thing or two from a thug
I call Roger in my head as we're bound
Together by the make-believe ring of crime

I'm worn out and my wrist has a cramp
Like a Tour de France cyclist I give up
The race and yet certain details foretell
I shall wear his crown but now surrender
To Mignon, a little drunk, as he plows
Into D in that chancy dawn that starts
Our tale, inside out, phantom frame

Having ascended high above the sea
Like a crow's nest from where D shakes
Her dust rag and bids adieu to ghosts
They find themselves tangled up
In the damp sails of an avalanche
"Boy, I was really wasted last night,"
He laughs taking in the scene

From the way he speaks, lights
His cigarette, D knows him for a pimp
Like a bird they say that flies
Into a serpent's mouth, she goes
"Stay, I mean, if you want to."
Among the stolen radio wires, shabby
Rugs and lamps, a life begins

As is the habit, Divine will hustle
On Place Blanche while Mignon
Takes in a show. Under his advice
She thrives, knowing whom to roll
And whom to blackmail in the daily
Protocol where coke lends a hazy hand
Bodies float, untouchable

I must insist on Mignon's looks
Undoubtedly a thug he carries
Bits of light that trail like ivy on a stele
A pedestal half hidden with flowers
He's been pissing on since boyhood:
Legs spread, knees slightly bent
"I've dropped a pearl," he says

Black eyes for most mac daddies
A matter of shame—for Mignon:
"My two violet posies" or when
The need seizes him: "I've got
A cigar at the tip of my lips."
D knows nothing yet about this
Business of ratting out her friends

To the cops. For now he keeps
His traitor mug to himself
It's not that he approves but
The caress is so much sweeter
Who's about to pull a job
The inspector asks—100 francs
In your piggybank, snap!

Stool pigeon that's me! Mignon walks
Down Rue Dancourt high on his own
Abjection lest its intensity kill him
Felt hat, plaid suit, shoulders back
His tie a flame and those outrageous
Yellow pointy shoes peculiar to macs
He steals their thunder, all smiles

After two stints in jail he imagines
The effect each new outfit will have
On the boys. Prison is a savage god
To whom he offers gold watches, pens,
Rings and scarves. He dreams less
Of strutting his stuff with ladies than
Entering a cell in a white silk shirt

Open at the neck. That is the shape
Of the fate he bows to, maybe since
He once read, scrawled in a john
A tag about *Martin the Faggot,*
Bob the Queer and *Li'l Meadow*
The Swish. It's hard not to wish
His name were up there, cursive temple

Of felons. Accursed would do more
Justice, I think—there comes a day when
One tires of the hero stance and snitches
To be back in the sandbox with other cast-
Offs, but for now Divine drinks her tea
Like a dove while Mignon, hands in pockets,
Does his cha-cha: three steps, shuffle and back

Each stolen object: liquor, perfume,
Fake jewelry, gives the room its
Mysterious allure like flashing
Lights on a distant ship. Parked car
Or friend's pocket, Mignon will boost
Anything anywhere and D will simply
Say, I feel like praying on his bare chest

On Sundays they go to mass, gold
Clasp missal in D's hand, clickety-
Clack they kneel on plush pews
And let a mean-looking priest
Cram the Host into their mouths
"Our Mother Who Art in Heaven,"
They pour out in unison, bow down

To the splendor of the pious world
At home, Mignon dives into D
As into a mirror—a silent key opens
The door and he becomes the sea
Monster then solid rock where
Andromeda, chained naked, must
Lie under a ravaged sky, mindful

Of the man who lets her drink
A sip of tea, lips pressed together
Pass it back to him, etc. ...
At the Roxy bar he likes to play
Poker dice, his gestures strike
A timeless pose rolling a cigarette
Uncapping a fountain pen

How sweet it is to speak
Of those two at the precise
Moment when planes are
Sobbing and the whole world
Is running amok before gun-
Fire. Already the soldiers'
Flesh droops like a half moon

While I dream of the lovers' garret
And the ways love surprises
People's lives like a walk-on part:
Two young wrestlers huddle together
Tangled hair, open shirts, they rewrite
The score high up in the Milky Way
Other constellations take shape:

Boxer, Violin, Dagger and Sailor
A whole new map of heavens outlined
On D's wall where she throws her cum
At the sight of a cherry blossom strangely
Black and stiff in its vase, D the farm girl
That she is, feels the cut like a murdered child
Mignon couldn't care less, gives a horselaugh

In return. Blows follow, land and slide
Softly. There's something off-putting to D
About fighting back, that grimace
Of a raised fist and knitted brows
Leaves her cold—too butch in a word
Like whistling with two fingers in your mouth
Or pulling up one's pants, both hands at once

Slang belonged to men, the queens liked
To think, intrinsic rights of a warrior
His crest and spurs. Fairies have their own
Idiom. One day standing at the bar, Mimosa
Dares, "His screwy tale…"
And pisses everybody off
"Broad acting tough," someone spits

Bit of tobacco caught between his lips
The argot that curls their tongues
Makes D weak in the knees, little gasps
Like a hand on a fly
Their pig Latin—eddbay, allbay—and derailed speech
"Go, you're cured," the pimps would say
Meaning all's well that ends well. Beat it!

At dawn, Divine hears church bells
And returns in her mind to a small
Rainy town three or four years ago
When, still Culafroy, he roamed the streets
And slept on a bench with other derelicts
All fraternal souls in the eternal dreary morning
Squeezed by destiny

The child that preoccupies us is invisible
Train stations or docks, cops see squat
Even in jail, he seems to have been smuggled in
Like smokes, razor blades or the air of a phonograph
Spellbound, the runaway kid can't sleep a lick
Walks around shadowy streets peering at cupids
And altars—such a gilded world in its magic wig

Next to Mignon's furnace body, D grows
Cold, remembering the young vagabond stumble
Against bums and debris while she sleeps
In the husk of their married selves
This morning, the ghost of my dream or rather
Its corpse, now no bigger than a king's epiphany
Cake, floats in the air, serene like a baptism

I go back to bed and wait for chow.
To enter the precise and tangible world
Of my cell is out of the question now
Mignon, Divine, I'm all alone here
True or not, you will have guessed
That in the end it's my own destiny's coat
I drape on D's shoulders—tatters or courtly mantle

As I dart around, turning D into a saint
The reader will have to improvise his own
Notion of time and duration. Beyond good
And evil, I take her by the hand and lead,
Poor angel that I am, toward luxury
D learns from the inside by touching
Like a blind man: marble, rugs, ebony

When her hired car passes by a wrought-
Iron gate or traces a silent figure eight
On the gravel, Divine is most an infanta
Up her sleeve, she carries a small fan
Made of muslin and ivory that she unfurls
Over her chin, flashing between two words
"He's dumb as a doorknob," Mimosa adds

A little tipsy, Divine's taken to the station
In front of a crowd scattered on the Boulevard
Lock'er up and throw away the key, they chant
Next day she's back to her spot, one eyelid
Blue and swollen. "Sweet Jesus, girls,
I about died the way those cops wiped my face
Like Holy Women"

Each bust is always the first I realize
As soon as my hands are caught
In their steel coupé
More dazzling than a theorem
The raw consolation 24/7
Of piss, formaldehyde and sweat
Beneath the coarse wool blankets

Divine and Mignon, to my mind
The ideal lovers. He a giant
Whose feet cover half the globe
His boner so huge and calm
Sexes slip like rings on a finger
You'd think young warriors, June 14th
1940, buggering us all as they march

In the dusty sun. I close my eyes.
For Mignon, D is barely a pretext
But for Divine he's everything:
Her joystick, little pony, love missile
Jesus in his manger, baby brother
An object of pure luxury that she decks
Out with ribbons and flowers

When Mimo pays a visit, she and D
Kiss on the cheek. "I just love your
Pad," she says, it's like a priest's home
All that green in the back. Must be
Sweet to sleep with those ghosts nearby."
The cemetery was like a liquid eye
In a black man's palm

It had entered D's soul the way certain
Phrases enter a text, a letter here, a letter there
At the window, Mimosa, looking for a grave
Yells out, "Bitch, you finally croaked, six
Feet under while I walk on your head, whore!"
Mignon, who's about to ditch D, looks around
A strange crumbly smile on his lips

Mimosa's man, Roger, had joined the army
She's gone to war, she had told Mignon
Who offered, for kicks, to replace him
And that was that. Our households, our
Loves don't look like yours. Without
Batting an eyelash nor a drop of remorse
He'd decided to split from D

Without wanting to spoil the effect
Let us come close to the scene
Where the treacherous queen
Tweets on as if she hadn't just
Plunged her dagger into D's heart
"When it's still inside and bulges
Along the crease that goes on and on

You'd think the Belle strolled off
A cruise ship, no kidding," she croons
Cutting her eyes at Mignon
Who steps into the puddle
Of their giddy fag speech
Like a jewelry thief, shadowy
"No news from your Roger man?"

"I'm the Quite-Alone," she whispers
Her ring finger holding at bay
An invisible storm: eyes, teeth,
Mouth, everything that has to do
With the exuberance of voice and gesture
Veiled and gloved in a mysterious sheen
Divine knows the score though she'll forget

At times to hold her tongue in front
Of the macs, Place Clichy, and Mignon
Will have to school her with two slaps
Ouch! She's no taller than the zinc bar
Scram! He's fuming under the green neon
The queens telegraph each other, "I'm the
Q-Q," meaning the Quite-Quite

Looking for a reason to quarrel
With Divine, Mignon finds none
Calls her a slut and leaves the attic
Now that she's alone, what will I do?
Shall I give her that gypsy kid, fresh
Off the boat, with his tall pumps and sailor
Pants that cup his butt like a public bench?

Let it be known we love without
Sacrament nor morals
Our laws are stitched in the raw
Malfeasance of the one who blows
A hole in his bridal bed after six moons
For fun, trailing behind him the immense
Aura of scorn for all square things, bonds, etc.

What I need now is to pull out the rug
From under D, watch as she falls and breaks
Her neck from mezzanine floor, or put
Another way, blow up her image
Then cut and press together into the sheets
Of my notebook when I'm good and ready
So that only a hint of her essence remains

Hence D's fan found in the hallway
By Mr. Roquelaure as he returns
With *Le Petit Parisien* and a bottle
Of milk. That very night Divine
Runs into Mignon quite by chance
Not a word about who ditched whom
Nor why. He whistles, a tad contrite

Mimosa flies up from nowhere
Her wild voice suddenly male
To D's ears: "Get the fuck out
You dirty whore, cocksucker!"
Mignon, splendid once more
In his cowardice which frames him
Like a white halo, stands aside

"Go ahead, kill each other,"
He says, "See if I care."
I still hear his mean laughter
Like a street fanfare
A showy rain of kicks and blows
Descends from top to bottom
Though most of D's end in the air

When all is said and done, life
Returns to normal in the ballad
Of Montmartre above the dead
Pity me! I'm pushing thirty
My head swaddled in romance
While I rot in the joint, God picks
Daisies for his mystic throne

In the game of self-contempt
I've become a master, gold
Medal hanging from a ribbon
Were I to say I'm nothing
But an old whore, who's to up
The ante on the table of tar and feather
Below which I lie lowest of all

Divine and I play by the same
Rules that make us don the fluffy
Boas and gaudy tinsel of a feeling
Separate from its truth. We simply
Swallow the injury and smile with
Our accordion mouths no matter what
Mignon-the-adorable-cheat does

That's the only way I can love him
Borne out of stone indifference
The very same sentence D will apply
To Our Lady of the Flowers
Who makes his formal entrance
Here, dear reader, through the back-
Door of crime where he waits

Like a bridegroom in white gloves
"Who's there?" the old man asks
"It's me," our 16-year-old replies
Strange how easy it is to kill
As the heart lines up straight in front
Of the weapon and the neck finds a resting
Place between the assassin's joined hands

The old man lies dead on a blue rug
I listen to the chimes that flood his head
You'd think the teen was running
From grove to grove on an April road
Orange blossom in his velvet buttonhole
Where the fuck does he stash his dough?
Our Lady pounds and scrapes in vain

In the midst of objects that have lost
All meaning, a monstrous sieve
Through which pass the dead souls
Of furniture. He panics. Get the hell
Out! The cops will be here any minute!
Just then he bumps into a vase: twenty
Thousand francs flutter to his feet

Air. Crystal. Nocturnal silence
He walks for all eternity, toward
A small hotel for tricks and johns
In the rented room he comes face
To face with that first rise of nausea
Many convicts have told me about
The dead man flows in your veins

Seeps out of your eyes, ears and mouth
Wild flowers bursting through a corpse
To shake off the stiff, really to vomit him
Our Lady holds himself, first light as a bird
Then his assassin's hand circles the crown
Hard. The night disappears at the rim of sleep
Let the young murderer be my haunted castle

Pilorge is the one I think of most
Sprawled out on the cover of *Détective*
Magazine. Face, somber like a forest
On a stormy night, you will need no ladder
To ascend the guillotine. The others are already
There: Weidmann, Sun Angel, Soclay.
I've dreamed my share of deaths

Our Lady of the Flowers comes
From the same wall stippled
With sun and shadow as fear
Stretches his limbs, gives his smile
A bluish tint and the sensation of floating
Impossibly svelte in that spectral gray
Flannel suit of his

He wore the day of the crime
And that he'll wear the day he dies
Right now he's at Gare St. Lazare
Buying a ticket for Le Havre
It takes him no more than a second
To realize that he's dropped his fat
Wallet and Mignon's picked it up

The sound of each bill as he counts
Under his breath and pockets ten
Squinting like a Chicago gangster—
That's his template or maybe a crook
From Marseilles—and then unbelievably
Returns the rest to Our Lady of the Flowers
I'll let you imagine their dialogue

Go ahead. Be my guest. Think the wildest
Schemes hanging on a thread of slang
They exchange in a brotherly embrace
Mignon orders a suit for both of them
Shoes and the whole nine yards that give
A man that special charm. Two small hoods
In search of gold cruising Avenue Wagram

And then one day, inevitably, Our Lady
Confesses his crime. Mignon returns
The favor with Divine, although he can't
Quite choke the old gag of ratting out his pals
Mixed in the silent drama of abetting
And a tender feeling for this teenage thief
Still the kid better explain his wacky name

Little by little he comes to it
With such strain that the marble
Serpents coiled in his face
Awake and the name enters the room
"You see, the guys used to call me that ..."
Mignon understands that the smallest
Sign even discernible breath will destroy him

Bowled over by his effort, the young
Assassin sinks into the vile mud
I'd like to transform into a bed of roses
Or better yet an altar bathed in light
Help! Mignon, Divine, Our Lady,
Stay! I cry waving both of my arms
But a terrible dream sweeps all cells

Like a giant crocodile made up
Of guards' mouths and judges' chests
And the poisoned air of jail
Swallows me whole very slowly
I appear before the judge, white
As a sheet on which I sign my confession
Sure that I'll be pardoned

What have I done? my lawyer asks
In shock. Was I nuts? No way
To take it back, undo the ball of twine
That traced the path from my icy cell
To the black corridors of the courthouse
Maybe I can seduce the guard who drags me
By the wrist? I'm as good as dead, my friends

At death's door, one foot in the grave
The sands of life are running out
At certain moments one truly grasps
What is meant by such expressions
The visceral vertigo that precedes
Falling from a precipice, everything
Goes black before the final shock

Not even a stony arm to catch me
And yet back in box 426 I drink in
The sweet fullness of my work
Its soothing comfort as if the mind
Deep inside was a footprint
I walk along inch by inch, transfixed,
Though I stumble more than once

Twenty thousand francs at the Palace
Won't last forever, Mignon must
Be thinking of returning to Divine
Now that their dough is gone
Dressed like two fake kings
Our Lady and Mignon collapse
Heads and shoulders at her feet

Divine, who until now has only
Loved macho guys, feels like a
New blade of grass is pushing up
From the earth. She falls hard
For Our Lady's flower face and
Begins the slow apprenticeship
Of masculinity

She whistles, hands in pockets
Imagines her arms and legs
On the body of a boxer
Striking a pose she builds
Like a puzzle, dashing from
Girl to boy. In the end, space cadet,
she forgets her lessons

To seal in the new switch
She dreams up a friendship
With a real pimp where each
Gesture is plain as a rock
Stiff bearer of truth
She'll name Marchetti
Assembled for the occasion

From an endless catalogue
Of thighs, torsos, knees and hair
She keeps ready for her lonely nights
If you read below the line you'll see
Each of these constructs hatched
By her desire, her hunger
Up close shows the same soul:

The very one she would've liked
To have. Once invented, Marchetti
Plays his part to a T, until one night
She pretends to be tired of Our Lady
And please can you take him off
My hands. They shake on it.
"No sweat!" One man to another

But instead of more virile
Divine just turns old, dry bones
Like an ivory crucifix beginning
To lose its sheen, she'll scream
If you turn on the light
The least shadow sends her trembling
Sirens' invitation to death

It's the season of tears
The way we speak of
The season of rains
The joy that signals
Suicide. Before you
Know it, she's blushed
For a yes or no

The-Very-Crimson turned on
By an adolescent! It's not the job
That shames her, after all, she's
Been drinking from that cup a thousand
Years, Miss Whore to you, good folks,
It's the little scraps others find harmless
That slice her veins and let the words

Fly from their coffins. Even as Culafroy
She dreads their power to bring her down
To the lowest rung. Let us steal a glance
At that era of Divine's life which holds
The immense Sahara of his childhood
Under a widening sun steeped in poison.
In short pants and schoolboy smock

He cries, sad little sovereign,
The makeshift violin that Ernestine
Refused to buy, all gone now
Nothing but broken white chords
And a broomstick handle, he's kicked
The whole lot under the floor from where
Thin specters of sound come to haunt his sleep

Everything about the village is strange
Like an invitation to watch a cortège
Of First-Communion girls with porcelain
Heads crowned in flowers and choirboys
Swinging censers under a noonday sun
Toward evening, one might see their elder
Sisters carry stillborns in narrow pine

Varnished like violin cases
Then at a crawl up a tree, boys
Would press their naked bellies
To feel the sap, all skin, earth, sky.
Rye, pine, clover stand upside down
In the moonlight lake. Divine's child-
Hood—at least some of it—looks like that

Let's say she's never feared God, Jesus
Nor the Holy Virgin, not like their wrath,
Contempt for her brand of loving
Until Gabriel makes the scene. I see him
Walking down a street, almost running
Bumping into D as the doorbell rings twice
Above the little candy store he's ducked in

I want to talk about those chance meetings
I provoke within the book like a surprise
Dollar package one buys for tots: that
Single instant when I glance at the busy
Street, a strange tenderness in my heart
I'm charmed. My gaze returns and all's
Gone. Thus, Divine meets Gabriel.

Like a cliff or glass wall his back
Arches, black wings of an eagle
Fly out above the shadows.
Gabriel is a foot soldier dressed
In sky-blue. We'll sketch him
Later when he stands off to the side
Of our story. Naturally, D will call him

Archangel. For fear of Mignon
She sees him in town and at once
Knows that he's a branch of her life
An underground vein. "You're not
My friend. You are my heart, myself,"
She says to him. He smiles, "Damn!"
Tickled pink by such worship.

All the way from Blanche
To Pigalle they walk as if blessed
In matrimony by the rabble
That twitters on their passage
Sick with fear the old queen
Dreams of war maneuvers
A parade in the forbidden city

It had to happen! One day she invites
Gabriel upstairs to rehearse a role
Equal in length to her longing: blinds drawn
She pretends she's just awoken. "Sit down."
His coarse wool uniform is a measure,
Even proof that she remembers the black cloth
Of country priests and state orphans.

"Doesn't that itch?" she asks. Later she'll say,
"Those pants, what a turn-on!"
"You're nuts! I got drawers on; the wool doesn't
Even touch my skin." Divine, I've said it
Before, is clad in blue which bends around
Her pale body like a tongue thrown in lament:
"I'm getting old, pushing thirty."

Gabriel has the courtesy not to flatter
Her with a lie: "That's the true age."
Two angels on a wire tired of flying
Now tossed by wind into a field
Of nettles couldn't be more chaste
But comes a night when the Archangel
Turns faun: he rips her open, half

Man half horse, their teeth part
Gleaming in the night, skin and eyes
Now lighter than ash or salt
D swoons with love like a nymph in a tree
Then whoosh! he's gone and dead at war
Buried where he fell by the Chateau
Of Touraine. She can visit his grave

In the narrow circle of her solitude
D wouldn't leave the attic for days
And nights on end; blinds drawn
On the Bay of the Dead, she lies
In bed drinking tea, feeling old—
Hollowed eyes, hair plastered
Under a wig—the queen can't help

To descend, in between fits of blue,
The strict periphery of her being
Until she finds what she's looking
For: in the childhood stream there
Stands Alberto with his heavy leather
Pouch, a puckering smile that D paints
With her own mouth

"You wanna touch'em," the Snake
Charmer says. "Go ahead, they won't
Hurt you," Alberto adds, showing
Three vipers writhing about, their dark
Heads a tangle of cowls, icy scales
Glistening in the petrified light
Like a spark, revelation falls on him

At the very moment Alberto's hand
Finds the hissing thing gliding under
His fingertips, suddenly more feeling
Than ever before like those tiny fleshy
Bumps the blind use to decipher Braille
It seems to Lou just then that he could
Swallow a whole mess of snakes as long

As Berto's hand doesn't leave his
Divine now shudders at the very thought
The long syllables of her boyhood name
Forever coiled in the maiden space that starts
Her knowing: an imperceptible trace, a cube
Of silence wild enough to blow up the church
God is hollow like Marie-Antoinette's plaster

Bust that sat on the mantle in the blue slate house
Or the little lead soldiers my cellmate Clément
Paints, minuscule warriors hard as corpses
That sometimes tie me down with their Lilliputian
Sad stories and then to get loose I have to offer D
In exchange. Thus I live with the mystery
Of infinite holes in the shape of men.

I've got to come back to myself, my life
As a convict, the veins, the bones of it
When really I'd wished for nothing more
Than to show you a book laden with flowers
Snowy skirts and pale blue ribbons. The world
Of the living is too far away, ghostly shreds
The poor country boys don at carnival

I'm haunted by signs: circles, orbs,
Billiards, Venetian lanterns, soccer
Ball of the goalie in his orange jersey.
What's the worst that can happen other
Than what will happen? And yet I'm scared
As if I were a cadaver pursued by the cadaver
That I am. Jackal, fox, the whole animal

Reign holds court down below
I need a dream, a poem to shatter
The walls of my prison. Swallows
Nest in my armpits, if you look away
For a second, a young murderer appears
A silk hanky in his buttonhole, he's just
Come back from a night of dives with sailors

And whores, and doesn't know it's his crystal
Flesh my eyes probe as if all those points
Of light traced a pontoon, temporary bridge
To an elsewhere so real my naked feet slide
On the freshly washed deck (what deck? you
Must be mad, there's nothing but flat stones
And the tears I mistake for roses). The end.

Meanwhile outside, Divine finds herself
In one of those narrow bars hurried by
The promise of a tryst. At the other tables
The queens all chichi and nasty tongues
Crane their necks to better see D's coronet
Of fake pearls. Judith bows to the floor
" My respects, Madame!"

"Up yours!" Divine shoots back.
"Die Puppe hat gesprochen," someone says.
As she bursts out laughing, the crown falls
And breaks. In the general mirth that ensues
"The D is dethroned!" "Sunk," "Fallen from
High On," "Poor exile!" On the sawdust floor
The little pearls look just like those we thread

Through miles of brass wire to make
Funeral wreaths, which in turn resemble
Those that lay around my childhood
Cemetery, rusty and busted, what's left
After wind and rain but a pink porcelain
Angel with blue wings
In the bar the girls sink to their knees

Only the men stand. Then D raises
A strange strident laugh and sudden
As a card trick rips out her dental plate
Only to set it on her skull and with a
Changed voice, lips eating dust, says,
"Get this, ladies, I'm still a fucking queen."
It took incomparably more soul to replace

The bridge back in her mouth.
How shall we explain that D is now
Thirty, same age as me, of course
From twenty to twenty-seven
There came a period of deep luxury
When she led the sinuously complicated
Life of a kept woman

There were cruises on the Mediterranean
A gilded hotel in Vienna, Venice, Rome
A Renaissance château and more
All this I imagine in such intimate detail
The vexations of my cell surrender without
A word. From time to time, D comes back
To us, noble châtelaine, she sends Mignon

Money-orders, sometimes even jewelry
He wears at night before fencing it
To treat his pals to a spread
Finally back in Paris she preens and ruffles
Amidst our gestures, thinks she strews
Roses and peonies like the village girls used
To do on the day of Corpus Christi

How is it possible that the blackest world
The most charred and dismal, the severe
Naked night of factory workers, their bodies
Bent by machinery be entwined with marvel
That very thing we call popular song lost in the wind
Where we touch words of such ferocious wealth
Their vowels slash like a ruby dagger, the way

They sing with grave mouths or maybe
Whistle, hands in their pockets, insouciant
The parts about ... marble steps ... garden
Of roses ... exquisite pink ... deep inside
I tremble before the jagged thorns and
Beauty bush that adorn them as if
They bloomed on a theater poster

Speaking of singing, of popular
Literature so light because unwritten
Flying from mouth to mouth so hungry
For those expressions we dream of using:
"Little shit," "monkey-face," "pretty thug"
In the twinkling of an eye we possess
The solid body of ten thousand hoods

Let it be said that runaway kids
All claim to have been mistreated
They know how to embroider this
Excuse with such singular detail
That everything we ever remember
From novels and news stories
About children kidnapped, tortured,

Sold, abandoned, raped and abused
Rushes at us and even the most suspicious
Folks like cops and judges will simply say
"One never knows."
For his fugue Lou invents a mean stepmother
They put him in jail out of habit
He's never seen anything so filthy

In a corner of his cell under a heap
Of dirty blankets, a kinky brown head
Laughs out loud: You AWOL from home?
Come on, you can talk here, we're among men
He shakes his brown rags which rattle like scrap
Iron. Help me with this leg, will you?
The little hoodlum had a wooden leg

Fastened to a stump with straps and buckles
Lou had the same aversion to infirmities as
He had for reptiles. The other kid frees up
A thigh and with a supreme effort
As if putting his hand on a flame
Lou touches the wood and finds himself
Clasping the apparatus close to his chest

The children sleep. As a species of
Punished outcasts, they are later
Transferred to a reformatory
Lou-Divine squats in his cell all day
And listens to the other little tramps
Whose vocabulary hugs shadowy
Alleys and scaled walls

Amidst this world of imps and fauns
The nuns float by like ballerinas
On poofy skirts and wag their heads
In silence
In spite of his tendency to daydream
He quickly becomes one of them
A vagabond picked up on the road

He doesn't want to disappoint
And lends a hand to a petty theft
When Mother Superior asks him why
Because the others thought me a thief
Is all he can say in response
The night swells above the hammocks
A jungle full of pestilence, stone monsters

From above, the dorm looks unchanged
Everything happens below the covers
Which seem to wrap around sleepers
In little groups the kids crawl out
And light cigarettes thin as straw
Draw up plans for escape, all doomed to fail
A secret kingdom of peers and commoners

A thousand little jabs with a fine needle
Draw blood and trace the most
Extravagant figures, this nocturnal
Tattooing, sacred hieroglyphs on white skin
Sometimes eyelids, armpits, even the soles
Of feet are marked with crude signs
Moons, snakes, boats and pierced hearts

It's the nuns' habits that suggest
An escape plan to Culafroy
Hanging in the workroom as they do
With stockings and coifs for nights
On end, they whisper as if they've
Done nothing else but hatch narrow
Routes of cutting loose

Please save your loud outcry
What follows is quite improbable
But truth is not my strong suit
Towards midnight two kids
Help themselves to the clothes
And step into the dark street
In their own wooden shoes

The peasants hardly notice
Maybe just a touch of wonder
At seeing these two short nuns
Their grave faces hurry along
On the open road
The sovereignty of hunger
Leads the way quicker than fear

I'm not done talking about D
In her attic between Our Lady,
Guileless heart of marble, and Gorgui
Whom she leaves together while
Cruising for old johns
Had she been a woman only
Little would she care but Divine

Is *also* a man. Easy to imagine
An afternoon picture show
Where hands touch in the dark
Later they'll get a beer and head on
Home. Crack! go the caps
She's strewn along the sidewalk
Under Gorgui's steel toes, sparks fly

All three are about to step out
A cigarette on each mouth
With a kitchen match D
Sets fire to her own stake
Lights up Our Lady's and holds
The flame to Gorgui
"That's bad luck," he says

She lets the match fall, now weary
Face all dark and skinny as a dragonfly
"You start with a tiny superstition
And end up falling in God's arms"
Or a priest's bed, Our Lady thinks
Without saying the words
Top of Rue Lepic lies *The Tabernacle*

Little cabaret I've talked about before
His Eminence is in charge—the very one
Who used to say, "I make'm cry every night"
Meaning the safes he jimmied with a crowbar
You'll find them all there but mostly Banjo,
1st-Communion, Agnes, Mimosa and Divine
And their gents

Under the low ceiling handsome butcher
Boys sometimes pass in floor-length gowns
The men play poker dice.
A phonograph and we dance
Nothing but giddy drag queens
Rubbing against teen pimps
A dreamboat for murder, don't you think?

Divine has dug up two silk dresses:
A black sheath with sequins
She will wear herself and a pale
Blue-faille with a bustle for Our Lady
"Are you nuts?"
In his eyes he sees his pals
Have a fit but none will snicker

Naked under the tight dress, he's captured
By the mirror, butt sticking out
Like two cellos
They're at the door
Spangled tulle fan and all
Let's just pin a velvet bud
On that tousled hair. There!

At the club it's a riot
Of muslin and flounces
Our Lady's buddies go wild
Between the downy skin
And the feel of silk
There's no telling how
He'll hide going hard

Under the stretched cloth
"Let me ditch this," he says
To Gorgui a little pink and wet
Around the eyes
Beyond them, the crowd rips
Like a sheer handkerchief
As Seck Gorgui—mighty

Thighs, shoulders rolling
Forward—clasps our killer close
Hands make a feathery nest
On his heart and off they go
On their flying carpet
Waltz, tango till dawn
Divine could cry with rage

A dragon or better yet a vampire
Strange how no one sees
Her front teeth lengthen nor the bony
Fingers scrape as on a chalkboard
But all nights come to an end
The trio walks into gray morning
Through a gauntlet of garbage cans

Like a raft slipping by
After a night of wine
Dance and laughter
They pass in shadow
Taraboom ti-ay
Taraboom ti-ay
Our Lady sings

In the strange logic of gender
It is always the denial that prompts
D to think none are women
Not even Ernestine her mother—
Save a little girl Culafroy
Used to know back home
Solange was her name

Out there on a stone bench
No wider than a hem
They sat together the same
Way—feet tucked, smocks
Pulled tight without a fold
Sometimes they'd go to the Rock
On days when the sky came down

Like blue powder in a water
Glass. Solange would say
"A year from now, a man will jump."
"What man?"
"We don't know. It's someone from far
He must be a hog dealer come to die
Away from the road."

After her convent and pilgrimages
The little seer turned up pretty
Much the same pale voice blond halo
Save she was no longer a part
Of his world; she'd become her own
Self like a work that long ago
Detached from its author

I interrupt myself "this morning"
To observe a spider weave a web
In the darkest corner of my cell
Having returned to the attic
Divine dons green pajamas
While Our Lady, elbows on knees
Smokes a last cigarette, a mound

Of mossy ruffles at his feet.
"Do you need help with this?"
Divine means the dress which
She starts unlacing in the back
Our Lady somewhat drunk
Lets her strip the prettiest part
Of his name

When he's naked he tumbles
Against Seck and D sees that
Today she'll have to settle
For the outer edge of the bed
That jealousy she felt on Rue Lepic
Worms its way leaving her mouth
Drawn shut like an alligator clutch

Gentle reader forgive me
If I skip the nightly mise-en-scène
Of their bodies pressed tight
At the gate of desire where D's
Cheeks admit entrance to tramps
Bandits and mercenaries without
Once asking "Who goes there?"

But in the final account
Divine rests her head
On the pillow knowing
Full well that the pair has
Played their game it seems
Without her. "C'est la vie,"
Say the old folks

In her deep misery
At being the odd
One out, Divine
Turns to archery and
Our Lady becomes
The burning bush
Of her invectives

I'm not going to keep
Those layabouts, she thinks
While drying her teacups
Hands grasp the axe, a streak
Of dreadful executions
A shock of mutilations
Appear out of nowhere

She drops her kitchen rag
And is back in the crawlspace
Of the human race, but one day
She's had enough; Seck had
Once again forgotten to include her
"Shit, I always think there's only
Two of us."

As so happens, D runs
Into Mimosa, old bat now
"Wowie zowie, I'm crazy
About your Lady
Still so fresh so divine."
"You like her? Want her?"
"Poor girl, she's done with you, eh?"

(Between them, queens
Always used the feminine
To speak of their friends)
"Our Lady's a pain in the ass
Stupid and soft to boot."
"So I can have her for sure?"
"Come to the house for tea."

"You know Roger's off
I'm the Quite-Widow!
You are so sweet, Divine
Let me kiss you, chérie"
Back home she lays out her trap
"Wanna make a hundred francs?"
"Doing what?" Our Lady asks

"Mimosa would like to sleep
With you, an hour or two
Roger's in the army …"
"Hell, that's not enough dough"
"Look, she's coming by later on
Make it last, you know the trick
But please don't pinch anything …"

Unaware of D's ambush
Our Lady lets the cat out
Of the bag: Gorgui approves
Seeing only the five louis
Reflected in his eyes like small
Miniature fields semy with gold
Still something eludes him

But the assassin is wilier
Than a snake in the grass
Territorial habit you pick up
Like a package or song half
Forgotten
The fact is Our Lady was back
Dealing coke for Marchetti

At times when I'm really down
I can't help but sing certain key
Phrases pimps invent behind
Closed doors. That kind of slang
Turns me inside out like a glove
As I pan with my sluice box
Amidst waste and gravel

For some reason it's Mignon-
Dainty-Feet I recall now
Walking into a department
Store as if pushed by a wave
Mirrors, chandeliers, carpets—
Sole luxury he can touch up close—
Mute the wild pitch of his heart

Another will, another self
Enter his eyes and mouth
Mignon the tough, the mac
Comes to life like a steep rock
Bright with mossy cracks
Where red-tailed birds fly off
In a stretch of sky above

He steals with art
Really, a science
The parabola arc
From showcase to
His pocket demands
Precision. Like falling
Asters or snowflakes

Perfume vials, pipes
And lighters trace
A short curve along
His thighs. Later
On the table he can
Hardly remember
Where they came from

"What have you stolen,
Young man?" a little old
Lady asks quietly.
The address flatters
Otherwise he'd make
A run for it and just like
That, the universe's upon him

The same day he's booked
Thieves, forgers, beggars
And pimps all led on a leash
As in a dream—Black Maria
Headed for Fresnes' house of arrest
I could without changing much
Speak of my life right here and now

At night, as soon as Mignon
Lies down on his bed
The whole prison goes
Topsy-turvy like a crepe
In a pan. His mouth
Is full of stones. Back
Home or in the attic

When he sits, rests
Or takes a cup of tea
He won't ever forget
That he sleeps or rests
On a carcass of a chair
The white tile latrine
The naked bulb that hangs

Dry kelp mattress, narrow
As a bier, chair fastened
To the wall with a chain
All hearken back to a very
Ancient order that shackles
The numb feet of His Majesty's
Galley slaves

Mignon had been in the pen
Three months when he heard
About Our Lady from a kid
In the parlor
Everything I will tell you, A to Z
He'd learnt by bits and scraps
Words whispered behind a hand

Spread like a fan.
Here's the scene:
Our Lady whose dealer
Moniker is Pete the Corsican
And the kid, hear the door bell
"Police!" one of the men says
Turning up his badge

One has to have a pixie soul
To mix everyday life—
Buttons to sew, laces to tie,
Blackheads to squeeze—
With detective novels.
The cops enter at once
Smelling crime

The fact is they're right
Because the kid's studio
Has the same choking air
Roses and arum lilies
On the mantelpiece
As when Our Lady
Strangled the old man

In the middle of the room
A naked body lay flat
The idea of a sham murder
Made the police ill at ease
Yet they quickly see the corpse
Is nothing more than a tailor's
Dummy

All they want is the coke
That one of their snitches
Has tracked down to the kid
"Give me the dope!"
He holds out a tiny packet
"What about him?"
"He's got nothing, chief!"

"What in the hell is that?"
A manikin. Divine's aura
Hangs like a scarf, absurd
And inexplicable veil.
One night the two kids
Had stolen from a parked car
A cardboard box:

Upon opening it, they found
The dreadful parts of a wax
Doll.
Fake or not cops take both
Back to the station: kicks
In the belly, slaps upside the head
Ribs and other places.

"Confess!" they scream
Finally Our Lady rolls
Under the table
Enraged, a policeman
Dives after him but another
Holds him back by the sleeve
"Let go, Gaubert. It's not like

He killed someone."
"That cute mug? he could
Do it, believe you me!"
Shaking like a leaf
Our Lady crawls out
From underneath
After all, it's just cocaine

"You're not going
To the guillotine,"
The good cop says
Handing him a cig
"The thing that pissed
Him off is your dummy."
Straining against his teeth

The murder confession
Rises in him like smoke
If he opens his mouth now
He's done for, sentenced
To death. I'm only eighteen
I can't die yet, he thinks quickly
God! No! Not a word!

He's safe. The confession
Pulls back like a tide
"I killed the old man."
"What old man?"
Our Lady laughs out loud
"I'm kidding, come on!"
But these people want to know

The detectives shout
Names from the last
Ten years—cold cases
Of violent deaths pass
Before his eyes—
It's a guessing game
"Am I hot? Ragon?"

A drowned child
On the shore
Undone
Incomprehensible
Face
"Yes! That's him."
Everything goes blank.

Overnight, Our Lady
Becomes a sensation
His name a household
Item across all of France
Under the rubric of thefts
Rapes and assaults with
A deadly weapon, the story

Makes the rounds, more
Hypnotic than the fly
Of a dead man
Three inches of print as if
Filled with bloody columns
And torture stakes
Paris won't sleep a wink

Tomorrow Our Lady
Appears in court before
The presiding judge,
Vase de Sainte-Marie.
Red draperies, ermine
Robe and high ceilings
The stage set for hearing

Since noon the room
Has been filling up
The crowd quivers
Shifts and shuffles
For the circumstance
Where Our Lady dances
On the lip of a chasm

Death here is but a black
Wing, a pirate's flag,
Green crêpe de Chine tie
Only visible evidence
Lies like a handprint
On the judge's desk
Stacked high with files

Between two Republican
Guards, the child enters
I dare to say all eyes
Read the graven words
In his aura: "I am the
Immaculate Conception"
Light gray flannel suit

Blue shirt open at the neck
And that rebel mop in his eyes
Any moment now a trap-door
Beneath the judges' feet
Would pull them down
Like fakirs hanging
For an eternity

The guard of honor
In hobnailed boots
Rattling bayonets
Appears on the left
Our Lady mistakes
Them for the firing
Squad

"All rise!"
"Your name is Adrien Baillon?"
"Yes, Your Honor."
" Born December 19th, 1920?"
"Yes, Your Honor."
"Can you give the court
The name you go by?"

Though the murderer
Doesn't answer
The name floats
Winged, secret and fragrant
"On the night of July 7, 1937
You entered the apartment
Of Paul Ragon, aged sixty-seven."

"Do you acknowledge these facts?"
"Yes, sir."
"There was no trace of forced entry
The report states, am I right?
Monsieur Ragon offered you liquor
And with this tie," the judge
Rolls the soft thing like an ectoplasm,

"You strangled the victim.
Do you here recognize
This as the crime weapon?"
"Yes, sir."
"And who gave you the idea
For such a method?"
"He did."

"The murdered man told you
How to eliminate him! Come,
Now, let's be serious!"
A sudden modesty prevents
Our Lady from speaking at once
"Mr. Ragon was wearing a tie
You see. It was too tight …

"So I thought if I was to squeeze
It'd be worser," and then barely
Loud enough for the first row
He adds, "cuz I've good arms."
"Good grief! but why, you wretch?"
"I was flat broke, strapped, beat."
The crowd blinks and twists

The twelve men of the jury
Leave through a small side door
"Chin up!" the defense attorney
Says to Our Lady. "You were
Frank and that'll count for us."
The kid's smile made the guards
Believe in God and geometry

The astounding story where
A fake murder leads to a real
One was now easier to accept
Since the manuscript I carried
In my back pocket had been
Stolen by the screw
Outside, snow's falling

One by one, witnesses
Are dropped into the trial,
Raise a hand and swear
"Nothing but the truth"
When Mimosa II steps up
A clerk shouts, "René Hirsh"
For First-Communion

Bewildered, Our Lady
Hears "Antoine Berthollet"
And so our little faggots
From Blanche to Pigalle
Are stripped of their frills
Like a paper flower
In a dancer's hand

The queens now showed
That carcass Our Lady guessed
Under the silk and velvet
Of each armchair
Whether timid or vamp
They no longer bloomed
At the outdoor cafés

Divine, Mimosa, 1st-Communion
Our Lady of the Flowers
How did faggots get these
Noms de guerre?
I didn't choose them at random
A whiff of incense and church
Candle seem to float here

As if I'd picked flowers from
The Virgin Mary's chapel
"Mr. Louis Culafroy," the clerk
Calls out. Leaning on Ernestine—
Only real woman there—Divine
Makes her entrance letting what's
Left of her beauty take a powder

"I do so swear," she too says
"What do you know about
The defendant?" the judge asks
"Your Honor, I've known him
For a long time. He's sweet
And childlike. He could be
My son."

For the first time in her life
She's taken seriously
In the human parade
The crowd grows restless
As a dog
Death seems to be late.
Finally the medical expert

Approaches the bench
His shifty voice hugs
Certain words: "Unbalanced,"
"Psychopath," "schizophrenia,"
"Freud … Jung … Adler …"
The great psychiatrist glances
At his notes

One gathers this: what's
A criminal? a necktie
Dancing in the moonlight
A vial of poison, gloved
Hands, sailor's blue collar
A series of benign gestures
The dagger that ascends the stairs

Silence falls on the courtroom
Our Lady thinks, "Maybe he
Ain't such a prick, after all."
He's granting his executioner
A premature forgiveness
Then it's the prosecutor's turn
One must protect our retirees

And send to death the children
Who slit their throats
It 's all well spoken
With a noble tone
The clock strikes five
"What can you say
In your defense?"

He wants to sound natural
But the answers come in slang
When he knows he ought to speak
French given the circumstance
And then a sentence takes shape
On his lips: "The old man was done for
Couldn't even get a hard-on."

The judge's robe trembles
Three times as if it were
A theater curtain
His defense attorney starts
Babbling about
Thirst and hunger
And the quasi-carnal

Temptation of the neck
He goes on and on
Totally off track
What game is this
Moron playing?
Safe in their seats
The jurors fall for

The corpse of a teen
Whose defense is still
Drooling, now begging
For reform school. We can
Barely hear him
Our Lady says in a sulk,
"I'd rather croak right now."

"Please, ladies and gentlemen,
He's but a child!" and to the kid
"Let me defend you."
Despair had entered him
Like an arrow and all that
Was left now were the white
Rags of his torn heart

He's no longer in
This room, this world
Bareheaded the monocle
Reads the verdict:
"Baillon, alias Our Lady
Of the Flowers, condemned
To capital punishment."

The jury stands up
It's the apotheosis.
Back to the guards
Our Lady seems
To embody the holy
Character of an ancient
Sacrificial victim

Goat, ox or child
Forty days later
On a spring night
The rig was ready
In the prison yard
At dawn Our Lady
Had his head cut

By a real knife.
Nothing happened.
Just because a god
Gives up the ghost
Doesn't mean the veil
Has to be torn
From top to bottom

I've reread my chapters
And notice that not a smile
Was given to Culafroy,
Divine nor the others.
In every child I see
I try to find the one I was
During visits I saw those

Two kids and loved them
For the men they'd become
On their shoulder blades
A ball of muscles already
Covered the tips of their wings
I looked at one's face and eyes
Thinking I could recognize

Myself when boom!
He smiled and no way
Could that be me, too pale
Like a loaf of bread.
Never had I laughed nor
Smiled for that matter and so
Crumbled before the child

Here are the last Divinarias
That you unravel
To read the essential form
Of a saint: her life?
The Valley of Death
With black stormy pines
I travel through in chains

Tic by tic, she detaches
From the human column
Having spent a lifetime
Plunging into the abyss
Now that her body's exiled—
Little bits of skin and bone—
She slips off to heaven

"Lady of High Pansiness"
She calls herself
Or Bernadette Soubirous
At the Charity convent
After her vision
Of the Holy Virgin
Madame, née Secret

Ernestine comes to
Divine's deathbed
And knows from signs
More obvious than a shroud
That only country women
Recognize: "He's leaving,"
She says to herself

Death was so close
That it could touch
D with its index
Finger as if knocking
On a door
But I'm not dead yet
She tells the priest

I heard the angels
Fart on the ceiling
And instantly sees
The old Adeline
Laid out cold on her bed
Culafroy with rigid arms
Lifts the sheets and dares

To kiss the icy lids
The thread starts there
That will lead Culafroy-
Divine to the end
Of course the shuffle,
Hobble and clumsy groping
Had begun much earlier

Here's how our Great
Divine dies
Looking for a gold
Watch that has slid
Between her thighs
Fist closed over
She hands it to Ernestine

Sitting at her bedside
Their two hands make
A shell with the wrist-
Watch in the middle
A vast calm descends
An almost liquid shit
Forms a lake beneath her

And she sinks
Ever so gently
Like a Roman ship
Into the volcanic
Waters of Lake Nemi
And heaves another sigh
Now tinged with blood

Then another: her last
Thus she passed away
One could say drowned
Ernestine who was waiting
Finally grasped that what
Was beating in their joined
Hands was the tick tock of the watch

Not being superstitious she lays
Out the corpse all by herself
Dressing D in a modest blue
Worsted suit of English cut
And there she is the Quite-Dead
White sheets like sails on a vessel
Drifting toward infinity

What possibly could I say
Now that she's no more
My cell so sweet today
Lulled by that kind death
What if I were free?
(Tomorrow the hearing)
Who will be judged?

A stranger whose name
Was once mine?
I can dwell until death
Amongst these widowers
Lamp, washbasin, broom
And the straw pallet
My spouse

I don't feel like sleeping
The wind outside gets
Fiercer by the second
Now rain adds its two cents
I should weep tonight
For my farewell
Rent, the exhausting fraternity

That links me to the dead
I shall live perhaps ...
And should I be condemned
To the stiffest sentence
I'll invent new lives
For the enchantment of my cell
For Mignon, Divine and Our-Lady

FRESNES PRISON, 1942

Ravished

Sois sage, ô ma douleur

—CHARLES BAUDELAIRE

I. Like a sentence stenciled in the sky

I see them dancing in the empty study hall
to an old radio show   windows

wide open   street sounds streaming in
blurred like a wet postcard on the asphalt

But what do I know?
Too much sense mars the writing

hollow space in my head
never heard a thing about her childhood

worth noting not even from Tatiana
It must be summer I'm only tracing

the faintest of lines a tennis court
at the end of August

stretches the minutes
before the grand dance is announced

you'll have to picture Town
Beach   almond cake casino

and a marriage proposal
maybe not exactly in that order

the right to error is a given here
Lola's parents consent

as per the old scroll
where sex and gender

wear the same robe
Michael Richardson's name chiseled

in even strokes   only child like a fossil track
we recognize at once

It's not the famous ball that causes
the collapse Tatiana says with that pensive

moue she takes crossing her legs as if
we had all the time in the world

if you want to know she's always
been like that even in school

never a tear   Pietà face   the heart
will come later   surely

Yes it seems like a garden
not yet planted   that region

of feeling one reserves for another season
When the rumors start about her engagement

Tatiana wonders who on earth could clasp
Lola V. Stein in his arms when all say

she's like water in one's cupped palms
sent rolling down the stairs

I'm convinced of nothing
in the half-light of doubt

a waiting room a puddle
we circle around, wobble

then come to a stop as if
on the brink of a ravine

That's how we'll invent the railing
that led to an awful night

The way I tell Lol's story, unreliable narrator
that I am, though my name seems to hold

the old gate standing in for the facts
won't be *once upon a time*

first nineteen years
running through the square

sprocket holes that
the projector teeth grab onto

I'll look for her just where I should
when she seems to move

as if in my direction
at the precise moment

two women step inside
the municipal casino

What to retain here save the scary
beauty Tatiana will have observed:

mouth   also height
aloft in the now emptying dance floor

Transfixed Lol watches   there's something
of a dead bird inside that black sheath

or maybe a slap she wears like a plunging neck-
line, a cormorant bordered by pale feathers

My story might begin here in that double layer
of tulle   the fiancé suddenly much older

moves toward   as if following a script
for an alternate ending

"I must invite her to dance."
The impulse so transparent so intense

they simply shiver at the peril
Already Lol loses her girlhood

smile   such agony
eyebrows knit ever so slightly

Anne-Marie Stretter finds herself
in his arms as evidence passes

from gaze to that naked space
on her shoulder   hand

caught in the acquiescent nod
of the first dance

It's behind the bar
its tall greenery

she understands the odd
code that excludes her

The ballroom's almost empty
and the couple strangely deaf

doesn't notice the music has stopped
that someone hurls insults

It's Lol's mother turning up
all trembly tangle of arms

looking for the exit door
in the charlatan light

of this dawn grown murky
carapace: please it's not that late

she yells to Michael Richardson
eyes on the ground they pass

before her, one after the other
like a sentence stenciled in the sky

II. Having forgotten the old algebra

When she can no longer
follow them through the gardens

Tatiana claims she simply
falls into a swoon, an absence

that will last several weeks
I don't know enough

to vouch for the veracity
that frames this shortcut

Drawn in like a subtraction
she stops answering

to her own name
such an insurmountable effort

rigs the room   floats
around   nomad thoughts

unrecognizable stretch of bed
face turned to the wall

Her extreme youth   you see
everyone said   would sweep

the blues away   lift like a high
tide the child's scowl

Over the silence she starts
asking for things: it's alright

to open the windows   eat
the news about their separation

her aptitude to remain calm
is judged as a good sign

the love she had stored
for Michael Richardson

was dying   a phantom
coach trailing dust and ashes

Having forgotten the old algebra
of heartache she steps out one day

into the sheer night   empty
boulevard curving toward

the outskirts   maybe
she'd been running

or else it was windy
when John Bedford spots her

he'll say later
pacing behind close enough

to see that arc of sadness
a pale shade of gray

slow slope   the blood
travels to the temples, hair

and mute hands that smell
like unused objects

he thinks slender
inexplicably young

fifteen at most
"You must be Miss Stein"

she nods several times
while he tells her askance

about himself: musician
aviation   happy

to make your acquaintance
the thud of words spreads

a net at their feet and so
like someone choking

coming up for air
she holds him tight

In my first draft
I have him kiss her first

but skip the way she returns
the parcel, lips touching

whole dark street hidden
in this meeting of strangers

John Bedford asks for her hand
in the vein of a certain grammar

that declines a broken heart
queer predilection for girls

left at the altar or gone mad
a requiem in B flat

One would describe the intimate
wedding in late October

and the wise precaution
not to invite any girlfriends

if I were writing an amusing play
with the appearance of truth

when all that needs to be said
is that Lol refuses to cite herself

and tarnish the perfect desert
that had been hers

III. Can I say "specificity"?

I regret not to provide a summary
of the ten years she lived in Uxbridge

and where she had three children: the line
between mimesis and repetition a mere thread

back and forth   a husband's
concerts abroad   flings

with young girls at his factory
bypasses choice   she simply

goes blank like a starched shirt
a little stiff at the collar

Bedford loves her just the way
she is he claims   that sleep-

walker rising in the morning
with golden hair   that silky

skin   silent and virtual
a quiver as he holds his wife

At this point of the *récit*
I harbor a fear

that would suspend the telling
a subsequent abyss in time

and space that effaces
can I say "specificity"?

At Uxbridge Lol imposes
a rigorous order on everything

rooms gardens pictures and vases
all seem faithful copies

of model homes seen
in store windows

obsessive and neat
she's imitating

quoting or rhyming
I couldn't say whom

In the long afternoons
when one bargains with

winter ice and shadows
the house's impeccable order

seems to rehearse a soliloquy
only the dead or departed get

Needless to say when they move
back to South Tahla, her parents' house

no less, she'll install the same
clocklike tidiness   matching

pathways in the garden
fanning out evenly

And then suddenly
the white syllables

which compose her
new habit: to go out

without pretext or reason
vanish into the dust

like sleep for all eternity
high heels click over

the dumb rocks angled
dead-end streets

IV. With a fist of ifs and maybes

Given the utter penury
of facts I'd be better off

cracking open vaults
melting gold links

than deciphering the inconsistent
script Lola Stein's life sketches

But like a hyphen between
knowing and unknowing

there and there
I continue my descent

with a fist of ifs
and maybes

There's only one room
left to redo   a couple

notices the fresh paint
gardeners standing by

no sooner than Lol
hears "dead, maybe"

she hides behind
a hedge   watches

the furtive kiss they steal
at the sound of a car

their lips part
anonymous again

then stationed in her garden
a little spot a nub a memory

the woman's gaze   walk?
a resemblance floats up in the dark

It's the words she must've heard
more than the likeness that trigger

her sorties in the streets
she moves during sleep

learns to walk far from home
as if borne by a sudden flame

Though I've followed her
more than once

she seems to recognize no one
and returns after each stroll

more dazzling and cheerful
in her transparent dress of oblivion

On rainy days she waits
out the insipid hours

that turn in place
a slow bonfire

Here's what I think
thoughts unleash step by step

the moment she crosses
the threshold   a vertigo

they come and go in a mad rush
always the same   until one

brighter than the others
manages to get caught:

the ancient ballroom shimmers
shipwrecked in the rain of South Tahla

That is why she walks
to better think of the ball

ripped out from inside
it grows and gets stronger

and then one day she enters
her true abode as if she'd known

no other   treacherous
headdress she adjusts

on this perdition road
A maniac, says Tatiana

stuck on the same key
can you imagine!

Indeed and I conclude
it's the exact moment

that extravagantly brutal dawn
into which the couple flee

Lol freezes and pinpoints
each fragile and graceful

second, captive in its own
bell, a refuge made of time

On this strait she rebuilds
the carcass of the world

powerless to change
its coordinates   the way

she sees herself at the center
really a triangle that fractures

with daybreak   sprung
miracle which would have

sealed all three of them
if only a bone-white word

had burst open, a gong or
dead dog on a beach, holey

flesh at high noon the absent
word nipped and trampled

awaits in the distance
still prodigious and unsaid

through which swims
the eternal film of Lol V. Stein

How to scale this impossible
boat aground and yet ready

to embark its three passengers
along a narrow future

which is now   inconsolable
place where the other body

as if in slow motion   breath
by breath   comes into view

while in a rigorous progression
hers disappears from the earth

V. As if stitching a sheet

As soon as she sees him
come out of the theatre

Lol recognizes the man
in the dark valley of her mind

something incendiary no doubt
rapacious leaps out from the eye

the way he looks at women
wanting more with each gaze

enough to recall
the one she'd known

before the ball?
Maybe she's wrong

What heat and fatigue!
She'd gladly slide

this heavy brooding
right here in the street

I see the following:
the man has a few

minutes to kill
before his rendezvous

scanning the boulevard
a vague hope Lol finds

divine
of meeting yet another girl

than the one she spied
in the garden

in tune with his step
she tails him at a distance

intent on placing her feet
in the same black prints

as if stitching a sheet
with big hasty needles

She must be wearing
those flat ballet shoes

I imagine or invent
a gray coat maybe a hat

that can be taken off
any minute to pass

out of sight   indiscernible
like a blade under the tongue

Roving eyes he ferrets
the teeming square

mourning every woman
in advance of the one

who doesn't exist yet
for whom he could

at the last minute ditch
the very lover they both await

Given the black and vaporous
mass of hair   that

small triangular face and
immense eyes outlined

by the ineffable guilt
of this adulterous body

given unlimited funds
of soft round hips

as she steps down from a bus
against the crowd

golden combs to the side
of a dark *voilette*

he will be the only one to free
in a single gesture that goes

snap around the shoulders
inside a miniscule cry

They are together—trains   winds
heartbeats   a summer solstice

come to as if pushed
by the same high tide

on the surface of an inlet
sensation of thirst misread again

Lol will have easily guessed
the name that trails there

spell or apparition
had known it for weeks now

the round vowel sounds
dance on pursed lips:

Tatiana Karl's migratory
beauty approaches the Forest

Hotel past waving alder trees
and a large naked field of rye

Sheets of ice one could say
where she'd gone in her youth

with Richardson   forgotten
about   crystal cup

she spins under her footsteps
No use to shadow them too close

since she knows where
they're headed

How she lowers herself flat
out barely visible dark stain

In milky green shadow
a few feet from the light

that just went up
on the third floor

At this distance she can't hear them
and only catches a glimpse

if one of them crosses the room
up and down a bluish shape

holding a cigarette
elbows on the sill

smooth as a stone
Tatiana reappears in the frame

Night has come mixed with lies
about a greenhouse on the edge

of town accounting for Lola's
return at such a late hour

Husband and children pity
her numb hands—can't help

believing her tall tale
almost lost the thread

VI. That is I, I'm afraid

In the frayed ledger
she will find Tatiana's address

and break the golden rule
of bourgeois custom

even though she knows better
than showing up unannounced

at the stone gate in the skin
of a white storm, a mere supplement

to her racing heart
"Lola, is that really you?"

Neither the hydrangeas already turning
purple nor the immense terrace

can hide Tatiana's surprise
while two men approach

a series
of gestures that go missing

the fact that Lol already knows
the one who almost staggers

and looks away from their kiss
"Ten years since I've seen you!"

In a strange contralto
Tatiana does the introductions

There' s an order one must execute
sounding out the correct pronouns

Holding Lol by the waist she presents
Doctor Pierre Beugner, her husband

and one of their friends, Jacques Hold
that is I, I'm afraid

During tea   permission to travel
through a region so ravaged and leveled

not a trace remains in Lol's façade
exchanged for banalities

about sprawl and traffic
then a zone of silence

the inherent truth one wishes
to conceal: she has nothing

to say
ten years at Uxbridge, a block

she reels off as if recapping a film
detached and precise though her eyes

hoard some knowledge
a cache of coins she fingers

whenever Tatiana leans back
or readjusts her hair

in the shallow hotel bed
As a matter of course

Lola's blondness—long
lustrous river she'd unpin

at night for the whole dorm
must be absent for now

What could she possibly want
this revenant from a passion so grand

they say she'd gone mad?
Of all the forgers I know

the least   my safe-conduct
astray with loose recollection

that dreadful escaping tendency
things—sketched in time—seem to have

"I could see the ocean from my window"
At once a red flag goes up the pole

of common wisdom
it's at least two hours by car

Nobody cares to correct the mistake
secretly glad her mind still sways

on this other plane
from time to time

In the sliding signifiers for desire
night falls like a dress

"Let's meet again, shall we?"
Lola suggests, ripe wheat

inflection in her voice
Near the door now she adds

as between two scores
"you must meet my husband"

Under the ornate chandelier
I separate the problem

into chapters
and verse

VII. Tossed from self to other

What happens next
at the Bedford house

is hard to explain even less
form a contiguous shape

that curves around the guests
                                    wavy and restive

balls on a pool table
about to break

It's a question of who sees
whom outside the fan

of windows skirting the grounds
The women are poised

by French doors   voices
loop together like an *étude à quatre mains*

In truth, it's the husband's violin
we hear bursting from the upper floors

Jean has a concert tomorrow
Lol explains   stroking Tatiana's hair

Something strange a sudden proximity
of opposites begins adrift

an arc that cuts flowerbeds
tears apart what's left of truth

I hide bent over to better hear
oh sweet venom

"Not sure I can visit as often
I have lovers, you know"

Tatiana's pink mouth pouts
velvety phonemes

In this blind man's bluff
it is Lola Stein who is "it"—we think—

and maybes
infinitely translatable

language   temporal and deictic
as "here" and "there"

When I look up again
from behind the bay window

Lol's eyes seek mine
belying a certain gaze theory

the consoling fiction men wear
like an armband

Here I am again stepping
into a bayou   deep mossy folds

where love changes hands and color,
over black and blue skies

On the periphery of her lie
I shall howl and be quartered

in the wide sense of the word
she utters to prove she's back among us:

"I've met someone recently"
Having just smelt a burning house

Tatiana feels like shouting, "watch out, Lola"
instead she turns towards Jacques Hold

"Shall we go?" He says, "no,"
like a convalescent stretching his long legs

VIII. Little blue planets

I feel like fainting
liquid mud in my veins

Whom did she meet
I wonder

"It's you, Jacques Hold"
she says using the formal *vous*

"You'd been to the movies
and I followed all the way

to the Forest Hotel where
she stood at the window

naked under black hair"
The sentence dies, empty

statue, its pedestal torn to bits
air heavy, despotic like a coup

She swallows my mouth
removes the game from its trap

and plucks my name again
"Lola Valérie Stein," I reply

In the burnt-out rubble
of yesterday

I am the man from South Tahla
We sink to the floor

deep inside a path around
land mines   eyes

little blue planets
blown out in a kiss

The violin has stopped
In its wake a crater

opens a plaintive trill
"I'll stop seeing her"

"I forbid you," Lola orders,
says it must be as before

I am to keep my rendezvous
on Tuesday, perpetual return

to the island of treachery
"And you, Lol, when do I see you?"

In free indirect style
she gives me the time and place

Even though it is three
in the morning

I park at the doctor's villa
tap Tatiana's door

She tiptoes where the floor slopes
wanting to keep up the myth

of the good wife
I'm quite sure Pierre Beugner

ignores nothing
of this chamber quartet

Tuesday in question
I'm in the hotel room

when I sense a gray shape
among the rye stalks

rustling
crepuscular ash blond

I know it is her
beyond a doubt

and begin to invent
she has seen me as well

Every lie integral
to writing this story

—approaching penumbra—
I block the scene

thinnest excuse to proffer
the third term   sweet

dogged self-exclusion
that Lola devours

between takes
while Jacques Hold

passes from front to back
"I" to "he"

pronominal
lover

who talks to another
still there on the edge

of a field   crowned
sovereign of her own making

I turn off the lights
a scent of rye follows me

back to town
then nothing

Pity the voyeur
who must traverse

a teeming square
plunge into a roiling sea

of faces
as if that's all it takes

to watch the one I stalk
like a man trying to make out

scrambled letters
at the margin of a night

I stop the car and follow
on foot   a knot at my throat

She's wearing that gray coat again
and a little black hat

knife or synonym
goes through me

How tall and slender
she seems   a kind of

practice for tomorrow
when we meet at a teahouse

She's already there
not even trying to lower

the flame that soars
of its own accord

barbarous insignia
part for whole

Suppose I now yowl
all the words in the book

coiled up
like a nest of vipers

"I've never waited,"
I start saying but she cuts me off

We're on the way, Lola adds
lifting her summer arms

as she spills out
of her sleeves and murmurs

"Tatiana?" We hug
the verdict

like the side of a wall
eyelids flutter   beads

of perspiration trickle down
"Can't live without her"

Won't she guess that I saw
her there sprawled in the rye

at the very moment Jacques Hold
explores a corporeal map

he knows by heart   arterial
white or blue lines mark the destination

of his hands but Tatiana Karl
has begun to retrace the same facts

about the dance at the municipal Casino
and how they all watched

that irrevocable blizzard
wipe out in a flash Lol's place in the universe

I sift her voice having lost her head
under the billowing sheets

an effect of decapitation
not escaping our interlocutor

Plain as a missed train Lol and I
sit on a bench unimaginable

currents drain all color
from our lips

carry off a last trace
of speech

IX. The long spoon of fear

That Lol is not yet "cured"
shows up in the way guests

hang on her words
when she laughs

too much or stops
mid-sentence

They pass the long spoon
of fear   ever so polite

not to spill a single drop
of the old belief

that women rarely come back
intact from such passion

All want to know more
about this act of translation

where one language
picks up someone

staggering
in an empty street

only to precipitate her further
into a gorge of substitutes

in the other—faint thumbprint
of alarm about her temples

Now radiant amid the seated
company   she draws

a pattern on the tablecloth
as if plants and meaning

shared a common plot
I look down at my shoes

any minute now the ship
will break into pieces

and I'll be swallowed
by the whale of a lie

But the moment passes
and Lol's husband drops

the stylus on a record
that sounds like rustling

skirts or footsteps
on dry leaves

I whirl Lola away
in a zigzag dance

toward the bay windows
"You went to the shore"

I say like a detective
coaxing a confession

Almost pitching
against my shoulders

—a cargo I've stolen before—
we'll go together, she says

tomorrow very early
meet me at the train station

Like a border guard
Tatiana takes up her post

but the noise of the phonograph
blurs our words—a fence

she squeezes through
on the edge of tears

She begins to understand
an intimation of things past

that a sudden explosion
has altered the grammar

that is to say binding agreement
between I and me   she and her

When Pierre Beugner appears
at her side I know for a fact

that should Tatiana cry even once
I'd be out of a job on the spot

Superb in her new dress of pain
she almost faints at the idea

as if death were a sheet
come to cover our nakedness

I invite Tatiana Karl to dance
"What does Lol mean when she claims

to have found happiness?"
Her hair cascades so close

to my lips I should start
running

Instead like every rake
I simply say, "Je t'aime."

X. Lost in the rye

Six o'clock   I'm at the hotel
ahead of Tatiana who I fear

will not come   the whole room
seems to know the color scheme

of suspicion spread out
like the clouds above

I want the gray shape
lost in the rye   asleep

an odalisque one might say
promised to her sultan

Against all odds Tatiana
arrives   red-eyed

folded into her grief
slowly she strips and lies

next to me amid the phrases
one uses for such instances

I stroke her hair which
has come undone

"It's that crazy Lola,
say it," she shouts to the bed sheets

In the darkness that floats
in the field caught on fire

we untie the anchor
let the vessel drift at last

XI. Scaffolding dawn

Sentenced to repeat itself
the train for Town Beach

would be empty at this hour
in its vertical

descent toward the sea
no mother to call Lol

mon petit chou
widely spaced trees

frame an open
canopy we glide by

like wooden horses
mounted on a carousel

I trace her name
on a window pane

as we approach
the sea resort

in the whining noise
of engine brakes

From here on I enter
Lola's memory vault

petrified wood
and fossil logs

we toss onto
layered rock

Arm in arm
man and wife

"You're now part of this trip
they kept me from"

"How silly," she adds,
"a thousand years have passed

and I'd recognize it at once"
With its milky white skin

frosty garlands and angels
cupolas and balustrades

the municipal casino
surrenders its arms

on the stroke of noon
It is not without magic

even if padlocked shut
and forsaken by gamblers

Lol sneaks a look
in every door   flushed

hair slightly damp
at the temples as if

stepping out of
the surf   a girl

from before
We start to laugh

past vitrines
holding tiaras and gowns

"Can I help you?" a little man
in black asks

A tiny peek, I explain
would do, you see

in our youth we came
here to dance

The ballroom appears
like a huge cruise ship

when its ten chandeliers
go up at once Lol cries out

I tap the man: a single switch
and darkness all around us

As if she were guiding my hand
to pen a letter I follow every curve

remember a curtained lounge
bordered by green plants

a blonde is roaring
with laughter   a mother screams

On the tracing paper of my mind
events overlap and condense

before the lovers descend
a scaffolding dawn

"Has it been long?" the custodian
wants to know

"Ten years," Lola replies
We are spared his recollection

A quick "I'm sorry" and we head out
into the vast tract of daylight

XII. Sous les pavés, la plage

Between tides her eyelashes
send shadows

across reeds and cattails
standing in slack water

sous les pavés, la plage
here meaning a shallow

band too silty for swimming
when we awake under hysteric gulls

ravenous to wring the neck
of this endless repetition

in which we lodge
without a lease

Further down a commotion
unspools around something

glistening in the sand
dead dog drawn like a cartoon

"It seems we'll have to
spend the night here," Lol says

"I'll call my husband
I've already told him it's the end …"

The sentence hangs
on her lips unfinished

points de suspension
implying a complicity effect

which yields to kindest
tears she laughs through

and always that glance
tips the scales

claims a room with a view
I pay tossing a few banknotes

One by one sky-blue fens
give in to the tide

that drowns each little set
erases their frilly partition

Lol inconsolable now reads
as the quotient of death

XIII. Like a cirque or bowl

What drifts before a dream
somber anatomy

cannot explain the quiet
fear in the air

Who goes there?
I have to undress her myself

eyes slide as if I were a stranger
turning a doorknob

" Police are downstairs," Lola says
stretched naked on the white bed

"Someone's being beaten
in the stairwell"

I do my best not to quarrel
having not paid the steep tariff

such history collects
She hardly knows me

abandoned phantom
I scale like a cirque or bowl

at the head of a glacier
trace flowers on its slopes

She moans in the reigning doubt
that I am Tatiana Karl's lover

Tremor   shouts and insults
hail down upon me   fast

metaphor of a hunted beast
careens in the space between us

Will you please tell me
who it was before me?

This spectral bed of names
Tatiana   Lola

remembers no difference
a palimpsest gone coarse

Night's knowledge
mixed with next moments

draws fingertips to the mouth
no longer clandestine

"It's time to leave"
Stepping out we mistake

the morning sidewalk
for a small body of water

Lola laughs at the mirage
"little canal in Venice"

On the train I press her
apart from unendurable pain

—*un grand blessé de guerre*
with his nurse—

to speak of Michael Richardson
as if suffering were a chain

of events she feeds me
scattering the crumbs

with her free hand
Just when she's tossed the last

bit about his voice
a suggestion of darker clouds

I ask for more   swept up
by the lurching train

Last passengers we alight
on the quay in a material

forest of sounds
half-saying goodbye

as if one could   for once
not return home

in the pulsing summer air
"Don't forget, Tatiana will be

waiting for you at the Forest Hotel"
her clacking high heels retreat

seeming to echo a movie still
the sight of which opens a chasm

• • • •

Night falls when I arrive
at the hotel

Lol's already there sleeping
in the rye stalks

shallow grave or subterfuge
inseparable from that bed

Acknowledgments

Molloy: The Flip Side was first published by BlazeVOX |Books| (Buffalo, New York, 2012). Its source text is the French edition of *Molloy* by Samuel Beckett (Paris: Editions de Minuit, 1951).

Our Lady of the Flowers, Echoic was first published by Les Figues Press (Los Angeles, 2013). Its source text is the French edition of *Notre-Dame-des-Fleurs* by Jean Genet (Paris: Gallimard, 1976).

The source text for *Ravished* is the French edition of *Le Ravissement de Lol V. Stein* by Marguerite Duras (Paris: Gallimard, 1964).

Endless gratitude to Geoffrey Gatza, Teresa Carmody, Vanessa Place, Andrew Wessels, George and Susan Quasha, and Sam Truitt for their support of my work.

Some of these poems appeared in *Absinthe*, *Bone Bouquet*, *Brooklyn Rail*, *Conjunctions*, *Eleven Eleven*, *Escape into Life*, *Jacket*, *Mirage*, *Quill Puddle*, the *Omnidawn blog*, *Supposium*, *The Offending Adam*, *Upstairs at Duroc,* and *Yew*. So much gratitude to the publishers and editors. You make things happen in the world.

Selections from *Ravished* were included in *women: poetry: migration: [an anthology]*. Ed. Jane Joritz-Nakagawa (Palmyra, New York: Theenk Books, 2017: 55–60).

Excerpts from *Our Lady of the Flowers, Echoic* were included in *Interventions: A Trans-Genre Anthology* (Ed. Roxanne Power. Santa Cruz: UP: 280–281).

The author wishes to thank Wayne State University for its generous support of this project through the Murray E. Jackson University Creative Scholar in the Arts Award and a Board of Governors Award. Special thanks are due to the Department of English and the Humanities Center.

About the Author

PHOTO: GEORGE TYSH

CHRIS TYSH is the author of nine books of poetry and drama. She holds fellowships from the National Endowment for the Arts and The Kresge Foundation. Her play, *Night Scales, a Fable for Klara K,* was staged at the WSU Studio Theatre under the direction of Aku Kadogo in 2010. With Oren Goldenberg, she has collaborated on a ciné-poem, *Alms of the Night.* She teaches at Wayne State University in Detroit.